NO IS A
BEAUTIFUL
WORD

OTHER BOOKS BY KEVIN HARNEY

BOOKS IN THE ORGANIC OUTREACH TRILOGY

Organic Outreach for Ordinary People

Organic Outreach for Churches

Organic Outreach for Families

OTHER BOOKS BY KEVIN AND SHERRY HARNEY

Leadership from the Inside Out

Seismic Shifts

Finding a Church You Can Love

The U-Turn Church

Reckless Faith

Empowered by His Presence

Pure genius! Say yes to this delightful and insightful study of no. It may very well change your life!

—LEE STROBEL, author, *The Case for Christ* and *The Case for Miracles*

This outstanding book is really not about saying no. It's about saying yes to what matters most. A gracious no is the gateway to purpose and priority.

—JEFF MANION, senior pastor, Ada Bible Church; author, *The Land Between*

This book reclaims the power of the most underappreciated word in the English language. This is a training manual on how to focus your life and priorities on the things that matter most.

—JOSHUA RYAN BUTLER, pastor, Redemption Church; author, *The Skeletons in God's Closet*

This book is easy to read, it's fun to read, and it hits so close to home. I'm innately terrible at saying no, but Kevin's chapters have convinced me I can be saved! I highly recommend it.

—JOHN GROOTERS, director, writer, producer, *Tortured for Christ—The Movie*

Finally, somebody says what so many of us need to hear. Our most precious resource is time, and priorities are the way we decide how to spend our time. And that means having the heart and mind to say no.

—MARK HORSTMAN, cofounder, Manager Tools; author, *The Effective Manager*

Reading this book has given us insight on how best to say no to others and also to each other without ruffling marital feathers. We have already put many of the nos to use, and they work!

—TERRY AND BETSY DAVIS, Tri-California Events

This book has easily made my list of top ten leadership books of all-time. Kevin digs into the issue that will have the greatest impact on your ability to maximize this one life.

—GREG KELLEY, CEO, World Mission

Kevin lives what he leads. In this book, he guides us into the secret of saying yes to a meaningful life.

—ADAM T. BARR, pastor; author,
Compassion without Compromise

This book is a critical read for anyone who struggles with busyness. It will inspire and encourage you to say yes to what really matters.

—BOB BOUWER, senior pastor, Faith
Church; author, *U-Turn Church*

Kevin Harney brings a fresh, creative, and long-overdue perspective on the power and importance of saying no. A must read for leaders and managers at all levels.

—SHAWN A. STROUD, colonel, US Army (retired)

Kevin's gentle queries and challenging ideas helped me make adjustments to live into the power of thoughtful choosing.

—SCOTT BOLINDER, executive director,
Institute for Bible Reading

What an incredible book! After reading it, I found I had more time for Jesus.

—MARK RISLEY, CEO and owner, Peninsula Sports

is a

BEAUTIFUL
WORD

HOPE *and* HELP *for the*
OVERCOMMITTED *and*
(*Occasionally*) EXHAUSTED

KEVIN G.
HARNEY

ZONDERVAN

No Is a Beautiful Word
Copyright © 2019 by Kevin G. Harney

Requests for information should be addressed to:
Zondervan, 3900 Sparks Dr. SE, Grand Rapids, Michigan 49546 ·

ISBN 978-0-310-58606-7 (softcover)

ISBN 978-0-310-58616-6 (audio)

ISBN 978-0-310-58607-4 (ebook)

Cover design: Juicebox Designs
Interior design: Denise Froehlich

Printed in the United States of America

18 19 20 21 22 LSC 10 9 8 7 6 5 4 3 2 1

To my father, Robert Terrance Harney,
who said no to me more than any human
being on this planet but also taught me the
glory, power, and wisdom of a strategic yes

CONTENTS

Foreword 13

Preface: A Thousand Nos 15

Introduction: The Buffet 17

PART 1:
WELCOME TO THE WORLD OF NO

1. No Definition . , , , ... 24
2. Every Yes Is a No 26
3. Every No Is a Yes 29
4. No Is a Beautiful Word 34
5. The Joy of No 36
6. God No 38
7. Positively Negative 41

   No Conclusion 42

PART 2:
KNOW YOUR NOS

8. Nos Aren't One-Size-Fits-All 45
9. No, Never, I'm Offended You Asked Me,
   and Don't Ever Ask Me Again 47
10. No, but Maybe Some Other Time 49
11. No, but I Know Someone 51

12. No, but I Have an Idea 53
13. No, but I Am Flattered 55
14. No, and Can I Give You Some Advice? . . . 56
15. No. Can I Tell You a Joke? 59
16. No. Can I Tell You Why?. 61
17. No, but I Love What You Are Doing 64
18. No, and You Should Be Careful 66
19. No, but Can I Offer You a Resource? 68
20. No, Thanks, That's Not My Thing 70
21. No, and This Could Cost Me 72
22. No, and I Never Will. 74
23. No, Because I Can't Decide 77
24. No, Because I Love You 78
25. No, but Please Don't Think the Worst . . . 80
26. No. No Comment! 82
27. No, Thank You 83

No Conclusion 84

PART 3:
PICKING YOUR NOS

28. Spare Your Nos 89
29. No Context 91
30. Scary Nos 93
31. Hard Nos 96
32. Dangerous Nos 98
33. No Gentleness 100
34. No to the No Monster. 101
35. Strategic Nos. 104

No Conclusion 106

PART 4:
NO STRATEGY

36. No with a Smile 111
37. No Margin 112
38. Telling Me No...................... 115
39. Telling You No 118
40. No More........................ 120
41. No Stalling 122
42. No Guts 125
43. Automatic Nos 127
44. No Apologies...................... 129
45. No Honesty....................... 131
46. Your Nos Will Define Your Life 135

    No Conclusion 136

PART 5:
CRITICAL NOS

47. No Morality 141
48. No Temptation 143
49. No Negativity 145
50. No Body 147
51. No Words 150
52. No Eyes......................... 153
53. No Seduction 157
54. No Time 160

    No Conclusion 162

PART 6:
NO RESULTS

55. No Understanding. 165
56. No Nos 167
57. No Fun 170
58. No Rest. 172
59. No Energy. .174
60. No Thinking 175
61. No Clutter. 179
62. No Priorities 181
63. No Way. 183

     No Conclusion 185

PART 7:
THE FREEDOM OF YES

64. Thoughtful Yes 189
65. Strategic Yes 191
66. Reflexive Yes 193
67. Let Your Yes Be Yes. 195
68. God Yes. 196

Closing Thoughts: Feasting on the Yes 199

Notes 201

FOREWORD

A retired man I met spends hours every day sitting in a coffee shop. He told me of a curious phenomenon about how people order coffee differently in the morning than they do in the afternoon.

"What do you mean?" I asked.

"In the morning they come in and say, 'I need a double espresso,' or, 'I need a skinny cappuccino.' In the afternoon, they say, 'I want a vanilla Frappuccino,' or, 'Can I please have a green tea without sweetener?' When it comes to caffeine, in the morning it's 'I *need*.' In the afternoon it's 'I *want*.'"

No Is a Beautiful Word is a book I need, not just want, and I suspect that will be true for many other readers as well. At first glance, learning to say no sounds so simple—just do it! Why do I need to read a book about it? But most of us know there are spiritual realities that make saying the word no a legitimate struggle. Kevin Harney resets the context of saying no by placing it inside a life filled with many beautiful yeses. He dissects the process of saying no so that you're equipped to discern when and how to apply the brilliance of saying no strategically and effectively. You'll find yourself saying, "Oh, that's a good idea," or, "I think I could say no *that* way."

After reading this book, I realized how essential learning to say no truly is. We will have happier, more fulfilling, more productive, more peaceful, and more God-honoring lives in direct proportion to how well we learn to say no. And we will open wide the door to numerous beautiful, enriching, and God-inspired yeses.

You will reap hours of time for every minute you invest in reading this book. You can't afford *not* to read it. The chapters fly by, but none of them will waste your time. They are laden with wisdom, biblical truth, and hard-won experience.

No Is a Beautiful Word is like that desperate morning cup of coffee. It's not just something we want. It's something we need.

—GARY THOMAS, author of *Sacred Marriage*

A THOUSAND NOS

I love words.

I enjoy writing. It's not my full-time job, but it's a delightful hobby. I can write for hours and have an absolute blast. Do you remember the dinner scene in the movie *What about Bob?* The main character, the likable but neurotic Bob Wiley, has crashed his therapist's vacation and family dinner. While they are eating, Bob makes loud noises of satisfaction with each bite of food. He can't help himself. He is in heaven.

That's me when I write. My wife tells me that when I am in my study working on a book or article, it sounds like I'm enjoying a good meal.

Because I love to write, every chapter of this book could have been longer—much longer. But as I wrote, I told myself no a thousand times. I cut words. I said no to extra sentences and paragraphs. I labored to make this book as concise as possible.

You'll find entire chapters that are one paragraph long. You may read some in less than a minute. Most chapters range from one to three pages.

Why are the chapters so brief? When I had written what I needed to communicate, I simply stopped. My goal has been minimum words with maximum impact!

Sometimes less is more. And with that, we're done with this preface.

THE BUFFET

You pick up a plate and begin the long walk down a line of seemingly endless food options. First you come to the salads. Potato salad, coleslaw, bean salad, Jell-O salad, kale and arugula, the traditional iceberg salad—even those strange, unrecognizable salads that grow only on buffets. You carefully scoop a couple of these "healthy" options onto your plate and continue down the line.

Next up, the starches and side dishes. The mashed potatoes and baked beans catch your attention and find their way onto your plate. Several vegetables are colorfully arranged in heaping piles, and you find a spot for some of them.

Then you notice the main dishes. They are eclectic and plentiful, culinary delights you've not tasted for some time. You take a few "samples" and carefully find a place for them in the growing mound on your plate. Nearing the end of this foodic marathon, you notice a chef cutting prime rib and steaming-hot turkey. You look at your plate, then back to the freshly sliced meat, trying to decide if there is room for just a few small slices. Of course there is! The meat and a dash of gravy just fit into that last space.

Then, out of the corner of your eye, you see the desserts. They are seductively presented, enticing you to come and partake. A piece of chocolate cake beckons and finds its way onto your plate.

Despairing, you know that you can't have it all. You've

loaded your plate, mixing several dishes together, filling and squeezing in as best you can. But there just isn't room. Your plate is full.

Whether you like buffets or avoid them religiously, you know what I'm talking about. It's the rare person who visits a buffet and walks away with one item. We all know that the goal of the buffet game is to get everything possible on your plate and walk it over to your table with the balance of an Olympic athlete, hoping none of it slips off.

There is an art to dining at a buffet.

Few have mastered it.

It demands superhuman restraint.

"Maybe I can stack one more item on this Mount Everest of food."

"Perhaps I can slide a small scoop of desert right there, on the edge of my plate."

"If only I had planned better!"

No matter how strategically you choose, there comes a point when the laws of physics prevail and there is no more room. Adding one more item requires removing something, or it will simply fall off the plate.

WELCOME TO LIFE!

There is a good chance you are reading this book because your plate is full. You can't add one more responsibility, help one more person, squeeze in one more meeting, or volunteer one more minute without something falling off. You may feel trapped or helpless. You may be dazed and confused, wondering, "How did I get here? How has my life become so full?"

So what *can* you do when your plate is overloaded? Is there any hope when you feel maxed out? And how do you prevent this from happening over and over again? Is there a way to rethink and reorder your life so that you don't get to this place?

The answer is simple: you learn how to say no. This tiny monosyllable can unleash joy, freedom, and power.

LET'S GET PERSONAL

Is your margin paper-thin?

Is your schedule jammed?

Is your mind weary?

Do you feel overextended and underappreciated?

Do you come across great opportunities you wish you could seize but feel there is no way you can fit them into your schedule?

Are less important things ruling your schedule while more important things pass you by?

Do you find yourself longing for more time, margin, peace, and productivity?

If you say yes to any of these questions, it is time to discover a simple but profound truth that has the power to change your life.

No is a beautiful word.

THREE THINGS YOU SHOULD KNOW

You should know three things before you read this book.

1. I wrote it for you. I'm serious. I have had hundreds of conversations over the past decade about the principles I am sharing in this book. I've talked with people from every walk of life—corporate executives, homeschool parents, military leaders, educators, law enforcement officers, students, servers at restaurants, flight attendants, doctors, nurses, entrepreneurs.

I've published several books, but writing this one was a

ten-year labor of love. I spent a year seeking to organize my thoughts in a way that will not only show you why you need to say no but also help you learn to love saying no. I address this book to you, the reader, but I have in mind real people who have been waiting for this book, people I love and care about.

2. *I wrote this book out of my life context.* Most of the stories and illustrations I share are examples from my life or the lives of people I know well. I want the ideas to be real and accessible. I know my temptations and struggles, and these are principles that have guided me in my decision making as an author, speaker, coach, pastor, husband, father, son, friend, golfer, student, and follower of Jesus. Yet while these are lessons learned through experience, I've written this book in a way that enables you to take something from each chapter and apply it to your life.

3. *I limited myself (most of the time) to one illustration or story in each chapter.* Sometimes when I read a book, the author uses three, four, or five illustrations to make the same point. I find myself skipping those "extra" stories once I understand what he or she is saying.

With that in mind, I want to say I trust you. I think you are smart enough to get the point with just one story. Once I've shared the key idea and illustrated it, I'll suggest a way you can apply it to your life, and I'll end the chapter.

You can read the book all at once, or you can read a little at a time. I recommend reading a chapter each day, taking time to consider the principle or idea shared, and then finding ways you can apply it to your life as you go through the day. While reading the whole book in one sitting will introduce you to its concepts, the book's real value is in your applying what you learn. As you do, you will begin to appreciate the beauty of saying no and learn to love the power of this word.

PART

1

WELCOME TO
THE WORLD OF
NO

N o!"
I hated hearing it. I avoided saying it. I thought it was a bad word.

Maybe you have some of the same reasons for avoiding the word no.

- "I don't want to disappoint people. I like to make them happy."
- "I feel bad when others see me as being unable to help."
- "I care about people, and I don't want others to see me as lacking compassion."
- "I don't want to be seen as limited or weak."
- "I don't want to be left out."

The list goes on and on.

But over time, something happened inside me. I discovered the beauty, the power, and the glory of a well-spoken and heartfelt no! I realized I was becoming more productive and found I was a happier person—a better person—as I learned to declare bold and consistent nos. Saying no at the right time and in the right way transformed my life.

As I entered the world of no, my joy increased. My purpose crystalized. My health improved. My relationships became stronger.

You may not believe me yet. But as I have shared these simple, transferrable, and life-changing ideas with others, they have experienced similar results.

Now I have the opportunity to share them with you.

Welcome to the world of no.

As you begin living in this world, you will learn to replace your weak yes with a strong no. In the coming hours and days (yes, it will happen that quickly), you will hear yourself saying things like, "No, thank you!" "No, I am not really interested in that." "No, my schedule does not allow that." "No, and I'm shocked you would even ask me." And, "Thanks for thinking of me, but I don't have the margin to participate at this time. I have to say no."

You can do this. It is not that difficult. Experiment. Dip your toes into the water.

It will take time. Practice will be essential. In most cases, it takes thirty days to form a new habit, to make doing something a natural part of your lifestyle, and this will be no different. Hang in there. Before you know it, your eyes will open and you will see a glorious new world.

1

NO DEFINITION

This book is not about placing limits on yourself or others. It is not ultimately about saying no. It is about making wise decisions and putting yourself in a place where you can say yes to the things that matter most. To do this, you will need to learn to say no, and say it a lot!

The more demands you have on your time, the more you need to master this powerful word. If the number of options placed before you seems to be growing exponentially, you will have to say no more frequently. If you don't learn to say this tiny little word, you will feel overwhelmed and exhausted.

Maybe you feel that way now.

Many people hear the word no and see limits. It makes them feel confined and trapped. They believe saying no will keep them from experiencing the richest and best life. They are afraid of missing out on excitement and new experiences. But these things are not true. Think about this: declaring a clear and confident no is a sign of wisdom and maturity.

A strategic no is not a negative or destructive statement. It is a creative one. By saying no, you are creating margin for an essential and life-changing yes.

This book is about learning to say no to countless bad things. But you will also learn to say no to many good things. You will learn to say no to hundreds of fun and interesting opportunities. And you will say no because good and fun can be the enemy of great and valuable.

When you embrace this truth, you can say no because you are committed to saying yes to what matters most. Here is what I want you to see as we get started: saying no is the mature and wise response to many of the options and opportunities that come your way (both bad and good). You will learn to speak this word many times and in many ways, not because you are a negative person but because you are committed to saying yes to the things that matter most.

2

EVERY YES IS A NO

A married father with two kids is living at maximum capacity. Between work and family, trying to be a good husband and father, his plate is full. Now, add to this his hatred of disappointing people and his love of having fun. He prefers saying yes and resists saying no. So when a buddy asks if he can play basketball one evening a week, he can't help it. He blurts, "Yes!"

What he fails to do is ask questions like, "What night of the week do you play?" or "How long do these games last?" He reminds himself that he works hard and deserves a bit more "me time." He says yes without reflecting on the implications.

Since his plate is full, things are already falling off. Commitments are being missed. Promises are being broken. Most of what he wants to do is good, but there are only so many hours in a day.

When he gets home and mentions the weekly basketball game to his wife, she asks, "What night of the week?" After a quick text message to his buddy, he informs her, "On Wednesdays." She gently reminds him that he picks up their daughter from dance class on Wednesday evenings and they spend some daddy-daughter time together. Also, their son occasionally has soccer games on Wednesdays.

A yes is not simply a yes. Saying yes to time with the guys means saying no to that one-on-one time he and his little girl have been enjoying after dance class. It means saying no to some of his son's games. In many cases, when important things fall off our plate, we don't even notice. Sadly, those are often the people we love most!

Saying yes to heading into the office an hour earlier every morning to get more work done can become a no to that exercise routine you have been trying to develop. Yes to purchasing a new toy might mean no to putting this month's college savings in the bank. Yes to taking a night class to further your education could be a no to a full night of sleep.

None of these yeses are bad, but all have consequences.

The question is, Are you being conscious of how your yes to one thing is a no to another?

IDENTIFY THE RESULT OF YOUR YES

The phone rang, and one of my publishers was on the line. "We were wondering if you could do some promotion for a new product you helped us develop. The curriculum has really taken off. It is booming in our national and international markets."

The publisher spoke some heartfelt words of appreciation for how both my wife and I had contributed to this project. Then he made the ask: "Would you be open to speaking to some leaders in San Francisco, LA, Chicago, and Michigan? We believe you would be an effective person to help influencers see how this product can impact their constituents in positive ways." I was intrigued because I believed in the message of the curriculum. I also knew I had no extra time. My plate was already full.

"This sounds interesting," I told him, "but I will need a couple of days to look at my schedule to see if I am able to cancel or move some things. I will also need to talk with my wife."

He chuckled. "Really?"

I was kind but clear in my response. "If I say yes to this, I will have to cancel a number of other things that are important to me. I have no margin. Can you give me a few days to see if I can negotiate this?"

He said yes, but I could tell he was still puzzled by my response. To his mind, this was an incredible opportunity, one I would be crazy to pass up. It was clear to me that he was not used to this level of personal analysis when it came to saying yes or no.

A few days later, we talked again. I let him know I would be willing to speak at a series of leaders' lunches in three different states. After we settled on the details, he asked about our earlier conversation and the way I had responded to his request. "No one has ever articulated that kind of thinking with such clarity," he said to me.

That led to a fifteen-minute conversation about the power of saying no and the reality that every yes is a no to something else. I shared the parable of the buffet from the introduction of this book and asked him how full his plate was. He admitted it was very full. "Then for you," I said, "at this point in your life, every yes is a no!" I encouraged him to evaluate what he would be saying no to whenever he said yes to anything new.

He thanked me for agreeing to present at these events. But then he was quiet for a moment and thanked me for helping him to understand that every yes is a no.

What about you? What is one thing you said yes to recently? Now think carefully. When you said yes what were the things you had to say no to?

CHAPTER

3

EVERY NO IS A YES

Ten thousand nos.

That's my best guess as to how many times I said no during the ten years I coached soccer for my three sons. Over a decade, I coached more than twenty teams, and that meant practices, Saturday games, drive time, team parties at our house, special outings to affirm the kids who had learned to juggle a ball thirty times or more without letting it hit the ground, being the referee at pickup games in our neighborhood, and giving lessons to my boys in our front yard. I said no again and again and again so I could say yes to my sons. I knew I wanted to be involved in and committed to this important part of their childhood.

"Hey, Kevin, can you golf on Saturday morning? We need a fourth."

"No. But thanks for the invitation! I am coaching three soccer games this Saturday. Maybe another time."

"Hey, Kevin, we have tickets for a hockey game on Thursday night. Any interest in coming along?"

"No. Zach has a soccer practice, but I appreciate the invitation."

"Hey, Kevin, we're going to our cottage this weekend. You want to come with us?"

"No. It's an AYSO [American Youth Soccer Organization] weekend for us. Have a great time!"

No. No. No. It's a mantra I repeat over and over. It flows naturally from the depths of my soul.

This chorus of nos crescendoes into an emphatic and powerful yes. Yes to making my sons a priority. Yes to consistency, even when it hurts. Yes to memories that have lasted for thirty years. Yes to a weekly declaration that my children matter more than my own interests and desires.

Was it difficult to say no to the countless opportunities and offers that came my way? You'd better believe it!

Were there times when I was tempted to bail out on my boys and their teammates? Of course I was tempted. But every time I said no, I was declaring a profound and heartfelt yes to my boys.

A STRATEGIC NO AND A NEW CAREER

I never aspired to be a writer. When I was in college, I enjoyed writing, but not all of my professors enjoyed reading what I produced. When I began working on my doctorate, I started getting invitations to write, and in some cases I was offered money to write articles, editorials, and studies. I wasn't paid much, but I felt honored that others seemed to enjoy what I wrote.

Some years later, as I was finishing my doctoral program, the largest publisher in my field of study asked my wife and me to write some studies, curricula, and even a few books. I was flattered, honored, and very interested.

Can you guess my dilemma? My plate was already full. I had no margin for anything new. I was working full-time and was immersed in research on my doctorate. We had three young and energetic sons, and my wife, Sherry, and I were trying to build a healthy, stable, and romantic marriage. I had no room on my plate to commit to something as demanding and rigorous as writing.

The best I could figure, I would need to carve out about twenty hours a week to do the writing projects the publisher was proposing. I knew that if I was going to take on this new opportunity, I had to say no to something in my life, and it would have to be something big.

I studied my schedule and evaluated my options. Like a bolt of lightning, it hit me. There was one thing I could remove, one existing commitment I could end that would allow me to say yes to writing twenty hours every week. I could declare one huge and painful no, and it would clear enough off my plate to make room for this new yes.

When I tell you what it was, you may think I lost my mind.

What was the big no that allowed me to say yes to a writing career?

Sports!

I love sports. I can sit and watch any sport and be transfixed. One Winter Olympics I spent several hours following the curling matches, drawn to the drama of teams pushing rocks gently down a strip of ice, sweeping madly and screaming at the top of their lungs. If curling can keep me glued to the television for hours, you can imagine what happens when football, basketball, soccer, tennis, or the dozens of other mainstream sports are on.

As I thought about my life, I realized I was spending an average of twenty hours a week watching sports, talking about sports, learning facts about favorite teams and athletes, and playing sports. I knew that if I decided to say no to following professional and college sports and participating in sports, I would have plenty of time to focus on becoming a writer. I also knew this would not be a onetime decision. It would be a commitment to say no tens of thousands of times in the decades to come.

Maybe to you the sacrifice seems too big, the no in this instance too severe. Or maybe you are scratching your head, wondering why this was such a big deal. For each one of us, it's something different. My love for sports might be similar to someone else's love for Netflix, cars, boats, or model trains.

The point is not the activity but the time it takes.

To be transparent, I knew that I could still engage in a few of my favorite sports (golf in the summer and snowboarding in the winter), but I'd need to cut out the rest. I also decided I could record the final round of golf tournaments on Sundays and watch them on fast-forward, skipping the commercials, and still have twenty extra hours a week to do my writing. Apart from these small luxuries, watching and following and partici- pating in sports would have to be off-limits.

This was my big no.

At the time, it was difficult, even painful. And it has required discipline over almost thirty years. But because I said no at that moment, and countless times over the next three dec- ades, I have been able to say yes to writing an average of twenty hours every week.

This has added up to around twenty-nine thousand hours of writing time.

My writing career is the product of thousands and thou- sands of nos. And what is the result of these sacrifices? I have been honored to write and publish more than ninety group stud- ies, ten books, hundreds of articles, and a number of curricula. Many of these have been written in partnership with my wife and other leaders I respect. These projects have been translated into many languages. Those thousands of nos are now positively impacting people all over the world.

Every no is truly a yes. And the decisions we make can bear fruit over a lifetime. But first we must learn that saying yes to something important means disciplining ourselves to say no to something else.

As you consider your goals and ambitions, is there something you've always wanted to do, but you never seem to have time or margin to commit to it? Don't let that dream die. Examine your life and ask, "Is there anything in my life— even something I love—that I'm willing to give up? Is there a no that can create room for a bigger yes?"

4

NO IS A BEAUTIFUL WORD

⸻※⸻

As children, we do not like being told no. We believe that freedom is all about doing what we want, when we want, any way we want. We believe that this definition of freedom leads to the best life possible. What we don't know is that declaring no can save our life!

"Hey, Mom, can I jump off the roof using my bedsheet as a parachute?"

"No!"

At that moment, the child asking the question feels disappointed. They think they are missing out on great fun. What they don't realize is that Mom is protecting them from a broken leg or worse. The word no can save lives.

"Would you like a slice of triple chocolate cake?"

Everything inside me screams, *Yes! A big slice, and a nice scoop of vanilla ice cream on the side, please!* My heart and my flesh want to say yes, but instead out of my mouth come the words, "No, thank you."

What they don't know is I am training for a triathlon, and I understand that this no, along with countless others, will impact my training and the outcome of the race. When I cross the finish line, there will be a sense of accomplishment that surpasses the momentary pleasure of a delicious dessert.

Saying no can add years to your life. And it can add life to your years.

No is a beautiful word. Maybe one of the most beautiful you will ever speak.

5

THE JOY OF NO

There is a freedom in saying no. No creates space, slows the pace, and saves face.

"Can you help out with the Girl Scout fundraiser?"

"You know, I believe in what you are doing, but right now I simply don't have the time to help. I can give a donation, but I can't be on the team that plans the fundraiser. I'm going to have to say no."

Once you make it clear that you can't invest time in weekly meetings for the next five months, you exhale a sigh of relief. You have retained your freedom. You won't have to lose an evening each week, a loss you can't afford at this time.

You know the feeling. Whenever you give a clear no, you feel a sense of peace. You've protected the joy level of your life. Because when a person is overextended, their joy evaporates, no matter how hard they try to protect it.

But there is the hard reality as well. The moment you say no (even if you say it diplomatically and graciously) is always difficult. No one finds joy looking into the eyes of an excited child and saying no. You don't delight in disappointing someone who wants your help or your involvement in a project. It can be painful to look into the mirror and say no to your own desires. But if no is the right answer, the result will open your schedule, grow your relationships, and bring peace to your soul. All of these things are gateways to a more joyful life.

CHAPTER

6

GOD NO

>———✴———<

Sometimes God says no.

Let's look at two examples. The first is silly and the other quite serious.

In the movie *Bruce Almighty*, Jim Carrey plays the title character, Bruce, who encounters God in the form of actor Morgan Freeman. God has decided to delegate his responsibilities to Bruce for a short period of time. As you can imagine, Bruce experiments with his unbounded power as he deals with an unending stream of prayer requests from billions of people around the globe.

Bruce attempts to manage the tsunami of prayers by setting up a filing system and then linking it to a database on his computer. In utter exasperation at the sheer number of requests, Bruce decides to hit the yes button and affirmatively answer every prayer request flooding his computer and his mind.

This would seem like a good idea, except thousands of people now win the lottery on the same day. They are expecting millions of dollars, but because the payout is split among all the winners, they end up with just enough money for a modest dinner out, leading to disappointment, riots, and mayhem.

Behind this humorous scene is a serious point.

God is not really concerned with whether we win or lose the lottery. He says no on a daily basis to the self-centered barrage of requests we make for easy money without work or responsibility. God is the wisest and most beautiful being in the universe, and he does what is best for us, even when we don't understand why. God does not always say yes to our prayers. He is far too loving to give in to self-centered prayers that cause more harm than good.

There is a fascinating account in the Bible of a day in the life of Jesus. It is found in Mark 1:21–39. Here we get a glimpse of how Jesus lived and loved. As the day begins, Jesus goes to a local place of worship and preaches. His power and authority amaze the people. Right in the middle of his message, a man who is spiritually tormented begins shouting out questions and making wild statements. Jesus silences him and speaks to the demon terrorizing the man. The man convulses, screams, and is set free.

After the worship service, Jesus walks with some of his friends to one of their homes, where a woman is sick with fever. Jesus goes back to work again. He shows love, care, and compassion by healing the woman.

That same evening, when the Sabbath time of rest is over and people can move about freely, a massive crowd descends on the home where Jesus is staying. This leads to a spontaneous time of compassionate service, during which Jesus heals the sick and frees those who are locked in the chains of spiritual bondage. Sickness is defeated and demons are sent running for the hills!

Very early the next morning, Jesus wakes up and takes a walk. He finds a quiet place where he can talk with his heavenly Father, but some of his disciples track him down to let him know that there are people looking for him. The disciples request that Jesus return to town and do more miracles and heal even more people.

Jesus says no.

He is crystal clear in his response.

Jesus knows there are still needs he could meet. He knows the people want him to stay and offer what only he can give them. He is profoundly aware that many will be disappointed if he does not come back.

But Jesus is committed to his mission. And his primary focus is not healing. He has come to be a teacher and a preacher. So Jesus says to his disciples, "Let us go somewhere else—to the nearby villages—so I can preach there also. *That is why I have come*" (Mark 1:38, emphasis added).

His response to the request is clear, simple, and mission driven. And it is an emphatic no. In his wisdom, Jesus—who is God in human form—says no to the urgent requests and needs of people so he can say yes to something greater, something better.

When we look back on our lives, I believe, all of us will be thankful that God said no to some of our prayer requests. I dated a couple of nice girls before I met my wife, Sherry, and there were times when I asked God, "Could this be the woman I will spend the rest of my life with?" God said, "No!" When I finally met my wife, I looked back and thanked God for his kind no. His no was preparing me for a better yes!

Jesus was "God with us" (Matt. 1:23). It was in his power to say yes to every request, yet there were times he said no. And if God says no, what does that teach us about the need for us to say no as well?

Take a moment to reflect on your life. Has God ever said no to something you wanted? Are you able to see wisdom in that no today?

If God says no, you can be confident that there are times when you need to say no too.

CHAPTER

7

POSITIVELY NEGATIVE

The word no is not about limiting ourselves; it is about setting ourselves free. It is not about what we won't get to experience, purchase, or enjoy; it is about the exact opposite! It is not about being cruel. It is often the kindest word we can speak.

When you utter a thoughtful and clear no, you are not being negative. You are actually being positive! It is time for you and me to become positively negative so we can live with freedom, peace, and productivity.

What is one no you can speak today that will make your life better?

NO CONCLUSION

NO REMINDERS

- The power of no is about learning to say no with strategic focus so you can say yes to the things that are most important and that hold the greatest value.
- When your life is full and your margin limited, every time you say yes to one thing, something else falls off your plate. When you say yes, you are also saying no.
- As you learn to utter strategic nos, you are freed up to say yes in a way that will revolutionize your life.
- Saying no can bring the greatest joy and value to your life. You must learn to say it and mean it.
- God says no. You can too.
- The most positive thing you might do today is say no.

NO EXERCISE

Find a quiet and private place, maybe your bedroom, a bathroom, or your car. Practice saying no. Let it come out of your mouth, and allow your ears to hear your voice saying this powerful word. Say it at least thirty times. You can vary the volume, change the tone, and even add "thank you." You can practice saying it with a smile and with a firm gaze. Get comfortable saying this word, because you will be saying it for the rest of your life.

PART

2

KNOW YOUR

NOS

Every restaurant has a menu. The menu can be simple, like the one at In-N-Out Burger. Burgers, fries, and drinks—that's it. Or it can be like the one at Cheesecake Factory, with page after page of appetizers, main dishes, salads, and desserts. Both restaurants have a menu, and the menu helps you choose which dishes you will eat.

As you are learning to say no, I want you to see that there is always a menu of options available to you. We tend to think there are only a few ways to say no. The menu of nos is much bigger than we imagine. There are many ways to say no, and in this section of the book, you will be introduced to a variety of them. This is not an exhaustive list. But it can help you learn to develop your own menu.

Once you have a good menu, you can choose which no fits each occasion. The starting point of this process is to know your nos.

Let's begin.

8

NOS AREN'T ONE-SIZE-FITS-ALL

---✳---

Each of us needs wisdom about which no to use in each of life's situations. Not all nos are created equal. Different nos fit different settings and people. They aren't one-size-fits-all.

When I was a child, I learned it is possible to do the right thing in the wrong way. There were times when my father would look at me and say, "Kevin, what you said is absolutely true, but you said it so poorly!" I had a sharp tongue and a quick wit, and there was often an edge in the way I said things. My father taught me the importance of learning to say the right thing the right way.

There are many situations in which the word no is necessary. Your challenge is to identify the correct no for each of these life circumstances and then speak it in the best possible way.

As you grow in conversational wisdom, you will learn many ways to say no. Choosing which no to use takes practice. One no might be perfect for a certain situation and with a particular person, but the same no may not connect as well in a different setting with a different relationship. For example, a friend might call and ask to hang out, but the timing doesn't work for you. A simple "No, but maybe some other time" would be appropriate. This no would not be the best response to a telemarketer pushing a product you do not need or want. There are some nos that will never work for certain people. Their personality or communication style is resistant. You will also learn that some nos are especially effective in certain relationships. Those nos connect and make sense to them.

Here is the key idea: You need to develop a diverse menu of nos. One size or type will not work in every situation.

Before you read on, think about four or five ways you say no. How could these various nos serve you well in different circumstances?

9

NO, NEVER, I'M OFFENDED YOU ASKED ME, AND DON'T EVER ASK ME AGAIN

She looked at me with seductive and inviting eyes. "Herr Harney, I would like to have sex with you if you would enjoy having sex with me." I was attending a community college just a short drive from Newport Beach, California, and it was the first day of my intermediate German class. In this surf town, many of the students (including the women) came to class wearing little more than bathing suits. I had never met this attractive blonde woman before, and these were the first words she spoke to me.

She offered her body to me. No blushing or blinking. She stood there waiting for an answer. I paused to process what I'd just heard. To be honest, I had never received an offer like this before. I didn't have a prepared response. When I finally spoke, my words seemed to shock her as much as her offer shocked me.

"No, I am not interested in having sex with you. As a matter of fact, I have a girlfriend and I don't have sex with her."

The California beach girl stared at me. I could tell she was appalled, as if I had just told her I eat baby kittens as a delicacy. She stammered, "Why?"

I assumed she was asking why I did not have sex with my girlfriend, not why I was rejecting her offer.

I took a couple of minutes to explain that my Christian faith led me to several convictions. One of these was a belief that the most beautiful context for sexual expression was in the deep and lifelong covenant of marriage. I told her I was committed to saving the joy and intimacy of sex for the woman I planned to spend my whole life with. She was taken aback but also intrigued.

When I look back on this surreal moment, I know that I needed a certain kind of no to convey my convictions. I was polite, but I also gave this young woman a forceful and clear denial. I let her know that I was not interested, that her offer was not appropriate, and that there was never any reason to ask me again.

As I've said, there is a menu of different ways to say no. My need for that situation was a no that quickly and effectively communicated my character and my values. I needed a loud and clear no!

As I walked away that day, I thought, *I am not the first person this woman has offered herself to today, and I will not be the last.* I was sad for her. But I was also grateful that I had spoken a bold, declarative, and emphatic no.

In case you are wondering, she got the message. She never made that offer to me again. When a person asks you to do something that falls utterly outside your moral convictions, you need only one response—a strong and uncompromising no.

Reflect on some of your convictions, boundaries, and moral absolutes. Prepare yourself to say no to anyone who tries to entice you to compromise in these areas.

10

NO, BUT MAYBE SOME
OTHER TIME

I was shocked when the word came out of my mouth. I had just delivered a lecture at a conference in San Diego, and the head of the Billy Graham Center for Evangelism was sitting in the room, listening. He approached me after the presentation.

"I love what you are teaching! This is a topic we have been studying at the Billy Graham Center, and you have developed some very helpful ideas. I am confident the work you are doing could be very valuable for church leaders and regional influencers. Would you be willing to come as a guest presenter and speak on this topic at the Billy Graham Center in Wheaton, Illinois?"

I didn't need to ponder my answer.

This man was offering me an opportunity to be a guest lecturer and train leaders at one of the top evangelism schools in the world. He wanted me to talk about a topic I had spent a good portion of my life studying. Everything inside me wanted to say, "Yes!"

Instead of accepting his gracious offer, I flatly declined it.

In this case, even though I declined, I said no with a caveat. I made it clear that I would be honored to do what he was asking of me, but I needed a couple more years to research, write about, and beta test the ideas I was developing. I told him I was very interested, but I did not want to risk teaching ideas I'd not yet put into practice. This topic was too important! I love the local church, and I care about how people reach out and share God's love. My heart breaks when I see outreach done poorly and inorganically.

The leader was gracious. He accepted my no, but he heard the caveat as well. He understood that I would be open to come and teach in a few years, and he thanked me for being honest and admitting that the ideas I had developed were not yet ready to be taught in that context.

Several years later, I received a call inviting me once again to speak at the Billy Graham Center. This time I said yes. The center was already using two of my books as part of their curriculum, and they wanted me to help them implement some of the ideas I had developed and written about.[1] I had spent several years testing the concepts in a variety of contexts with a broad cross section of people. I felt confident I could help leaders and churches with reproducible principles rather than risk hurting them with undeveloped, unpracticed ideas.

Sometimes the best no is simply, "No, but maybe some other time." I've had times when I used this no and nothing came of it. That's a risk you must take. But remember this: When you say no, you can leave the door open for a future yes. If you do this politely, your no indicates your interest but also gives clear reasons why now is not the right time.

Can you think of a time you said no to a request that was premature? How could you have exercised wisdom by saying, "No, but maybe some other time"?

11

NO, BUT I KNOW SOMEONE

———※———

After I had been editing trade books and reviewing manuscripts for a publisher for a few years, the publisher asked me to edit an academic book. It was written by Alister McGrath. I enjoyed working on this academic text and found it rewarding. Unfortunately, my plate had begun to fill up with some new writing opportunities. The next time the publisher called with an academic project, I knew I did not have the margin to accept. I had to say no.

In this situation, I selected another distinct and helpful kind of no from the menu. Rather than just rejecting the work, I offered a bold suggestion.

"Thanks for the opportunity, and I'm honored, but I simply don't have the time to do the quality of work I know you need."

I could tell they were disappointed. But before the conversation ended, I offered them an alternative.

"I know a young guy who I believe would do as good a job as I could . . . maybe even better!"

I had their interest. I told them about Ryan, a leader with a keen scholarly mind and an amazing understanding of the topic of the book they wanted edited. As I extolled Ryan's qualifications, I built a bridge between my publisher and this potential freelance editor.

Not only did they hire Ryan for the project, but he ended up doing a whole series of editing projects for them in the ensuing years. And over time, this gifted young man was hired onto the publishing staff and eventually became the editor of a three-book series I wrote.

This particular no has incredible creative power and beauty. When you say, "No, but I know someone," you do a number of things. You build bridges between people. You solve problems on both sides. You meet needs. And you create goodwill, as long as the connection you make is a healthy one.

Because this is a powerful no, I am very careful when I use it. You should be too. If you make a recommendation and it does not go well, it can reflect badly on you and harm the relationship you have with both parties.

This is a no that should be used with wisdom and sparingly.

When you say, "No, but I know someone," you need to be confident in the person you recommend. You want to be sure this is going to be a healthy relationship, a benefit to both of the people or institutions you are connecting.

CHAPTER

12

NO, BUT I HAVE AN IDEA

⁎⚯⁎

"Can you and your wife write a book for us?"

A friend in publishing had come to us, early in our writing career, with a proposal. They had a book idea and wanted to know if my wife and I were interested in doing the project. The working title was *Finding a Church You Can Love*. It was intended to be a short, practical book designed to guide people through the process of finding a local church that would best fit their needs.

When Sherry and I heard what they wanted, we gave an emphatic no! We explained that this philosophy of finding a church would encourage myopic and self-centered people to see the local church as a vendor of religious services, existing solely to please them and meet their wants and needs. This did not line up with our understanding of the purpose of the local church. We declined the offer.

Then we suggested what we felt would be a better idea.

"What if you expanded the book and had two sections? The first half would be about finding the right church for you. But the second half would focus on what you could bring to the church." We suggested a new title: *Finding a Church You Can Love and Loving the Church You Found*.[2]

The publishing team went back to the person who had developed the concept and presented the new idea. They loved it.

A short time later, the team came back to us and asked if we would consider writing the repurposed book. This time we gave an enthusiastic yes.

If we had simply said no, the book might not have been written. Or it might have been written but would have lacked balance, and we certainly would not have written it. When we said, "No, but we have another idea," it opened all sorts of new possibilities.

We have given away hundreds of copies of this book, in both English and Spanish. Whenever we meet someone who is looking for a church, sending a child off to college, or seeking to be more engaged in their church, we are glad to give them this useful resource.

Sometimes you should say no, but you may have an insight that will make something better. Have the courage to say, "No, but I have an idea!"

13

NO, BUT I AM FLATTERED

You will get offers you know you can't accept, but they make you feel good. When you receive this kind of invitation, how will you respond? I would suggest you smile and say, "No, thanks, but I am truly flattered that you would think of me. That means a lot."

14

NO, AND CAN I GIVE
YOU SOME ADVICE?

M y wife and I sit on the board of an international mission agency called World Mission.[3] This organization does many wonderful things, but its primary focus is distributing solar-powered audio Bibles to people in some of the poorest places in the world, where most of the population does not read. The vast majority of the people in this part of the world learn by listening.

At one of our board meetings, we watched a new video that the team wanted to roll out as part of their development strategy. The goal of the video was to help people see that some areas of the world have greater need than others, and we should allocate our time, energy, and financial resources to the places with the greatest needs.

The goal was noble and made perfect sense.

As we watched the video, I was struck by the beautiful artistry. It touched the heart and communicated the message with piercing power. When the video finished, we were asked for our input. Should we use the video in our communication with friends, constituents, and potential supporters?

I was the first to respond. I affirmed the fine work that had been done and the effectiveness of the video. But I said no. I did not believe the video was ready to share with a general audience. However, I asked if I could make a suggestion.

I was told this would be appreciated.

I pointed out some statistics used in the video that were surprising and dramatic but were also a potential off-ramp for the viewer. I shared that when I hear statistics, I am immediately skeptical, knowing they can be easily manipulated. When the statistics are dramatic and serve the purposes of the organization or person presenting them, I am even more cautious. I advised that some people who watch the video might stop paying attention to the message if they are distracted or find themselves questioning the statistics.

After I expressed my concern, several other board members entered the conversation and agreed. The board asked the team to edit the video, focusing less on statistics (even if they were accurate), and then bring the video back for one more review.

The revised video was far more powerful. The advice that the board members shared sharpened the message and removed potential distractions for those who would watch it in the months and years to come.

It would have been easy to say, "It looks great! Send it out." The video was well produced, dramatic, and interesting. But in this case, a few of us said, "No, it is not ready. If you let us give you some advice, it will be stronger."

Sometimes we offer a polite and respectful no followed by a clear suggestion on how to make something a yes. This type of no may take some additional time. It usually demands conversation, compromise, and more work. But in the end, it is worth it.

Don't be afraid to take the risk and say, "No, but can I offer you some advice?" Your input may be a blessing in disguise, leading to far better results.

Think about a time you gave a quick and easy no when you could have added some good advice. If you face a similar situation in the future, how can you expand your no to be more helpful?

15

NO. CAN I TELL
YOU A JOKE?

A man walked up to me. His eyes locked on mine, and I could tell he was frustrated.

"Harney, I know what you're doing!"

I played innocent. "What do you mean?"

His expression grew more intense. "Every time you make a joke and get people laughing . . . I know what you are doing!"

I smiled and gave him a wink.

I was pastoring a church, and every year we had a congregational meeting. At these gatherings, there were always a few people who liked to use this opportunity to bring their complaints and rile others up. It was usually the same people trying to create dissonance and bringing a negative spirit to the meeting.

One of them was bright, articulate, and quite contentious. Whenever he would get up to speak, you could feel the level of tension in the room increase. The church was filled with wonderful, loving, and peaceful people. This guy was an exception. He liked to nitpick and was constantly trying to light the fire of criticism.

My response, whenever he spoke, was to listen and then make a comment, joke, or observation that would get people laughing. I tried to keep things light when he was attempting to stir up strife, and this was strategic. It was my way of letting him know, "You are not going to co-opt this meeting and spin things negative." It was another way of saying no, in this case to his efforts to create a climate of antagonism. And I did this with humor. Through the years, I have learned that when people laugh, it is difficult to maintain a contentious atmosphere.

When this man stood up to speak, I did not say, "No, and may I tell you a joke?" With my words, I rejected the tone and the spirit behind his comments, standing against the climate he was trying to create.

I said no by keeping things light.

He was a bright guy, and I knew he knew what I was doing. My smile and wink let him know that I knew that he knew, but I didn't care. I was not going to let him take a great moment of celebration and turn it into a time for sowing discord!

When you say no and then tell a joke and get people laughing, you can change the spirit of a room or a conversation. Use this type of no sparingly and with wisdom. If you are not naturally funny, be careful! But if you have a good sense of humor, use it. A no and a joke can be a powerful combination.

16

NO. CAN I TELL YOU WHY?

A very sweet young couple approached me after a church service on a Sunday morning. They explained that they were new to the area and had been visiting a number of churches. With evident joy, they said, "We have decided to make Shoreline our church home!"

I was delighted. There are many wonderful churches in our community, and I consider the other pastors friends. But I'm still glad to hear when someone feels they've found a home in the church I pastor, and I'm delighted when they are ready to engage in the life of our congregation.

The husband looked at me and kindly said, "Now that we have decided to join this church, we would like to set a date to have you and your wife over for dinner so we can get to know you better."

I paused and said a silent prayer, asking God for wisdom as I spoke. I also prayed for this couple to accept what I was about to explain to them.

I tend to err on the side of honesty, and as my wife has reminded me many times over the years, I can be too direct and blunt. So I've learned how to soften my words to express greater kindness while speaking the truth. I carefully explained that I would not be able to set a date for dinner with them.

They looked shocked, hurt, and a little surprised.

I told them that our church has more than eighteen thousand people in our database and more than six thousand people who regularly engage in the life of the congregation. My schedule simply does not allow me to set dinner dates with every family in the church. I tried to lighten the moment by saying, "If our church had just one thousand families, and I had dinner with two families every week of the year, it would take about ten years to have dinner with everyone."

I knew right away that they came from a relatively small church and were disappointed by my no. Most churches in America have less than a hundred people, with fewer than fifty families. A pastor could easily visit with a different family each week, spending time in the home of every church member over the course of a year.

At our church, this was not possible.

The couple listened closely and then said, "Thanks so much for explaining that so clearly. It really makes sense, but it does make us a little sad." We went on to discuss the beauty and value of being part of a small church, where everyone knows everyone and the pastor is much more available to all the members. We also talked about the benefits of a larger church, one that provides a wide variety of ministries and programs for the community and church members.

I asked them if not having my wife and me over for dinner was a deal breaker for them. They assured me that it wasn't and said they were excited to get involved in a church that was different—and bigger—than any they had attended before.

If I had just said no without explaining why, it would have

been deeply hurtful and confusing for them. I had to say no, but that no was followed by a wonderful conversation, and they learned more about the church they were joining.

When you have to say no, add a simple explanation. It can go a long way in clearing up misunderstandings and faulty assumptions.

Think about a time or situation when you said no but didn't really give a reason. Think through how you might say no in the future but also explain why.

17

NO, BUT I LOVE WHAT
YOU ARE DOING

I have a dear friend who owned one of the largest trash companies in the United States. He had recently retired and sold the company. He is kind and generous and has a passion to use his resources to make the world a better place.

He serves on numerous boards and is committed to supporting a wonderful variety of causes he believes in. My freind has no shortage of opportunities to give financially and share his wisdom with other leaders. People are always knocking on his door, looking for advice or help.

When my wife and I founded a nonprofit organization, I decided to form a vision advisory team, a group of eight to ten couples and individuals with wisdom in law, business, finance, and international commerce.[4] In assembling this team, I started by laying out the expectations. Members would be asked to commit to pray monthly for the work of the organization, to offer leadership insight and suggestions each quarter, and to gather once a year for a one-day retreat and business meeting.

I asked my friend to consider being on this team. He took time to think, pray, look at his schedule, and weigh his options. Then he told me his answer.

No.

I not only appreciated his process and his answer but also loved the way he shared his no with me. He expressed how much he loved the vision of our newly launched organization. He spoke about how much he appreciated my friendship. He wanted to hear updates on how things were progressing. But he made it clear that he simply did not have the margin to take on another responsibility at that time.

I was not hurt or offended by his response. While I would have loved to have him on our team, and while I know we would have benefited from his wisdom, I respected the way he said no. It proved that he took this request seriously, and his response honored me. His kindness and affirmation were a positive encouragement, even though his answer was negative.

18

NO, AND YOU SHOULD
BE CAREFUL

Y ou are out on the town and run into a friend you haven't seen for a few months. After the two of you catch up a bit, he pulls you aside and lowers his voice.

"I got wind of an amazing investment deal that could pay off triple or quadruple what the market is paying. Do you want to invest?"

You can feel it in your bones. Something is askew, a little off. Deep in your gut, you know that anyone who puts money into this scam is going to regret it.

So what do you say? Try this on for size.

"No, and I would encourage you to be very careful!"

You can't tell your friend what to do. At the same time, it is completely fair, grown-up, and gracious to give him a warning. Look him in the eyes and say something like, "You know, everything in me says this could be a scam. For what it's worth, you should think long and hard before you invest your life savings in this venture."

Don't wait until a year or two later, after your friend has lost his life savings, and tell others, "I knew that was going to happen!" Love your friend enough to say something now. Have the courage to give him a warning. Humbly raise a red flag and say, "Be careful."

Anytime you have a warning light flashing in your mind, don't be afraid to say no. And be careful!

19

NO, BUT CAN I OFFER
YOU A RESOURCE?

It is rare that a month goes by without someone asking me if I can help them with a book idea.

"Kevin, would you be willing to read a manuscript I am working on and let me know what you think?"

"I have a friend who really wants to be a writer. Would you be willing to meet with her and give some ideas about how she could get into the world of publishing?"

"Hey, is there any chance you could bring my manuscript to one of your publishers and see if they will take a look at it?"

I once had someone ask if I could meet with her friend to coach them as a writer, edit their manuscript, and then deliver it to one of my publishers. I did the math and said, "Do you realize that you are asking me to do about forty hours of work for someone I have never met?"

I pressed ever further. "Is your friend planning on hiring me in a professional capacity, or are you asking me to donate a week of my time?"

I felt the question was fair, so I asked.

I could tell from her expression that she had not really thought about the significance or the cost of what she was asking. When I spoke that specific no, it led to a rich conversation. In the end, she apologized. She said, "I would never ask a friend who is a plumber to spend three or four days doing volunteer plumbing for a stranger. I don't know what I was thinking when I asked you to do all that work for free."

I told her that I get requests like this frequently and that most people underestimate the work it takes to review and comment on a manuscript. I explained that I had to say no, but I could offer a resource for her to share with her friend.

Several years ago, I wrote an article summarizing my best suggestions for those who want to learn how to break into the world of publishing. I mentioned this article and that it was on my website for free.[5] I assured her that this resource could help her friend, but this was the full extent of what I could offer.

People will ask you to do all sorts of things. And many can be helped if you point them toward a useful resource. This is not a lack of care. You aren't blowing someone off or treating them poorly; you are exercising responsible time management.

I'll leave you with one final suggestion. If you find that you often get the same questions or requests, consider whether there is a way you can develop a resource—an article, a booklet, a video—even if it simply offers advice on where to get more information. You will help people see the beauty in no if you complement your answer with a resource to assist them.

20

NO, THANKS, THAT'S NOT MY THING

So much in life is a matter of taste and preference, your personal likes and dislikes. It is not about right and wrong but about subjective enjoyment. So when someone asks you to engage in something you don't enjoy, and you don't want to do it, tell them.

Explain that it is not your thing.

Imagine someone invites you to a musical or a symphony, but going to these kinds of shows is slow and agonizing torture for you. What you really love is "professional" wrestling. How should you respond to your friend's invitation to the sympony?

Just be honest. Say no thank you. It probably won't end the friendship. And if your honesty does cost you the relationship, it wasn't much of a friendship to begin with.

Here is why I recommend being honest. If you say yes and act like you really enjoyed the local civic theater's production of *The Music Man*, you can bank on being invited to next month's production of *Little Shop of Horrors*. You might even end up getting season tickets for Christmas.

Be kind and diplomatic. But be free to say that you don't enjoy something. Some people love spending an afternoon tasting wine. Others spend their evenings at a twelve-step program. Some love physical activity—challenging hikes, off-road cycling, any new activity that tests their endurance. Others like sitting on a beach under an umbrella with a cool and refreshing beverage.

We are all different. You can remain friends, even good friends, and not have to enjoy all the same things.

You will save all sorts of misery if you learn to look someone straight in the eye, smile, and say, "No, thanks! That's not my thing."

21

NO, AND THIS
COULD COST ME

---※---

Some nos have built-in consequences. I live on the Central California Coast, an area famously known as wine country. The making, storing, selling, and enjoyment of wine is a big deal in my part of the world. I have close friends who really love talking about wine, tasting wine, smelling wine, looking at wine, tasting more wine, and then talking about it some more.

They really enjoy wine.

I have no problem with this, but I do have a problem.

I don't drink, ever.

I'll share about my history with alcoholism in the next chapter, but here I want to highlight one challenge I regularly face living in Central California wine country. Some of my dearest friends occasionally take day trips centered on wine tasting. They also have dinners at which drinks are paired with each course of the meal. These are fun social gatherings.

In general, my wife and I are not invited to these get-togethers.

The people organizing and hosting them know that we don't drink, so inviting us doesn't make sense.

We know that once we tell someone about our decision not to drink, there are consequences. There are events and gatherings we will not be invited to attend. We are mature adults. We get it. We fully understand. And we know that we will miss out on some fun times with dear friends.

But here is the key idea: this is a natural byproduct of saying no. While saying no brings freedom and allows us to express our deepest convictions, some nos have a price. We must recognize this and accept the cost.

The good news is that quite often, you'll discover surprising ways to still enjoy the things and people you love, even when you need to say no. One of my buddies has a well-stocked wine cellar, and whenever we are at his home with friends, we end up down in the cellar hanging out, talking, and drinking. He knows that my wife and I won't be trying his wines, but he always keeps a few bottles of nonalcoholic carbonated apple cider for us. We can enjoy a beverage, conversation, and fun with friends and still hold to our commitment not to drink alcohol.

Take a moment to reflect on a few nos you say that come with a cost. Remind yourself why it is still worth saying no, even when there are consequences.

22

NO, AND I NEVER WILL

I was thirteen years old when I quit drinking alcohol.

I was not a heavy drinker before that, but I would occasionally partake in some beer and wine. When I was thirteen, my granny (my dad's mother) sat me down. I knew this was going to be a serious conversation.

"Kevin," she said, "your dad drinks too much, and I worry about him."

Then she gave me a family history lesson. I learned that my dad's father, her first husband, had died as a drunk in a gutter in New York City. She continued, telling me about his father (my great-grandfather), who had died young because of damage to his liver from abusing alcohol.

My granny looked me straight in the eye and begged me to break the cycle.

"Promise me you won't be the fourth generation of men in our family to damage or destroy your life with alcohol." With tenderness and strength, as only a grandmother can, she laid out her request. "Will you promise me that you will never start drinking?"

I told her that I had already tried alcohol, but at that moment, understanding the past and out of love for my granny, I promised that I would never drink another drop for the rest of my life. I knew it was a bold commitment for a young teenager, but I made it. That was more than four decades ago, and I have kept that promise without exception.

Here is the irony. I have no idea whether my physiological makeup would have propelled me into the world of alcoholism if I had continued drinking. And I will never know.

On that day, I used a rare form of no, the "No, and I never will." This is a no of deep commitment. In addition to keeping me from the pitfalls of alcoholism, it has honed my ability to say no in other ways. I get offered a nice glass of wine on a regular basis, and I have learned that having an absolute and universal no in your life can make it easier to say no in other areas as well. Saying this type of no teaches you not to live on the fence. It's something I never have to think about; the answer is always a clear no.

Of course, the best result of this perpetual no is that I have never struggled with alcoholism. That family history of addiction has ended with me. I am a fairly passionate person, and when I love something, I love it a lot. Anyone who knows me can tell you of my obsession with spicy Mexican food. I don't just like it, I love it!

I've often wondered how my life might have been damaged if I had consumed alcohol with that same passion. If I drank beer like I eat burritos, I'd have a serious problem.

I quit drinking more than forty years ago, and I have said, "No, thank you," to offers of alcohol hundreds if not thousands of times. And here is my point. There are some nos that need to be absolute, rooted in a deep and uncompromising commitment. And when you make that decision, it gets easier as time passes to say no, because you know what your answer is going to be every time. I have decided in advance: "No, and I never will."

You may need to make a few of these unbending, premeditated nos in your life. If so, make the decision and then put your mind on autopilot. Resolve that when it comes to certain things, you will always say no.

23

NO, BECAUSE I CAN'T DECIDE

There will be moments when you teeter on the edge of a no or a yes. You will have a hard time discerning which answer is right for a specific situation, invitation, or opportunity.

Suppose a friend asks you to join them on a vacation, but you just can't seem to decide and you must make the call. What if someone asks a favor, but you are really on the fence about doing it? How do you respond when you feel pressure to serve on a committee but are not sure if you have the margin or time?

I would suggest that your default answer in these moments be a cautious no. In most cases, if you give an answer and then change your mind, it is easier to start with no and circle back and say yes. It is almost always more difficult to say yes at first and then come back and say no.

When you can't decide but must make a decision, just say, "No, thank you."

24

NO, BECAUSE I LOVE YOU

I was sitting in a restaurant with one of my sons. He was about five years old, and we were enjoying some good one-on-one time. As we were waiting for our meal to arrive, I found myself distracted by the drama unfolding just a few tables away.

A little boy was clearly out of control. He was loud and rude and was bothering everyone in our section of the restaurant. His mother was ignoring him, doing nothing to tame his wild behavior. I tried not to stare, but it was difficult to look away.

I did not realize my son was also watching this drama. He was studying me as I watched the boy and his mother. After a minute or two, my son poked me to get my attention.

"Dad, why doesn't that mom love her son?"

It was a strange but insightful question. I was a little surprised, so I asked him a question to clarify what he was thinking.

"Why do you think that mommy does not love her son?"

He responded right away. "If she loved him, she wouldn't let him act that way."

I agreed with him. We had a wonderful conversation about how dads and moms who really love their kids must say no. We all need boundaries, and it is not loving for a parent to allow a child to get away with horrible behavior, in public or in private.

The lesson is simple and clear. At times we need to say, "I love you, so I must say no."

As you look at your life, are there some nos you need to begin speaking because love compels you to do so?

25

NO, BUT PLEASE DON'T THINK THE WORST

A friend of the family was telling me about how she was handling what she called "an awkward relational situation." She and her husband had struck up a new friendship with another couple. They really liked them, but this couple loved going out to restaurants for dinner, and they kept asking my friends to join them.

My friend told me, "When we get home from work, the last thing we want to do is go out for dinner! We like being home, cooking our own meals, and having dinner as a couple." She went on to explain, "I just keep trying to come up with new excuses for why we can't go out for dinner with them."

I was confused. "I thought you said you like this couple."

"We do. We just don't like going out for dinner." She said her plan was to keep making up excuses until the dinner invitations stopped.

I told her that this might not be the best way to build a new friendship. "Your new friends will figure out you are just making excuses. When they do, they will think the worst. That's what human beings do."

"What do you mean?" she asked. "What will they think?"

"My guess is that they will think you don't like them. They will assume you don't want to spend any time with them. They will conclude that you really don't want to be their friends."

My friend seemed surprised. She was just trying to get them to stop asking for dinner dates.

I suggested she call them and explain that going out for dinner was not really an option because of their busy days and the rhythm of their evenings. She looked at me and asked, "Do you think that would hurt their feelings?"

I assured her that telling the truth would be far less hurtful than leaving a blank slate for these new friends to fill in with reasons that would be much worse.

"What kinds of things do you and your husband enjoy doing with friends?" I asked.

"We love to meet and play cards or board games *after* dinner," she replied. "We also enjoy Saturday hikes. We often do weekend breakfasts with friends and really enjoy that."

She followed up by calling these new friends and explaining why dinners out did not work for them. Instead, she offered a list of things they *would* enjoy doing in the coming weeks. This removed the potential for wrong assumptions and led to a blossoming new friendship.

When you have to say no, take time to explain the why. This keeps people from imagining the worst!

26

NO. NO COMMENT!

Y ou have experienced it. So have I.

Someone asks you a question, and you carefully explain why your answer is no. Sometime later, the same person asks the same question, maybe in a slightly different way. You say no again, and again you explain why. They seem to understand. But then, to your surprise, the same question comes up again. You begin to wonder if you are speaking clearly. You wonder if there is some way to break through and help them understand that your answer is simply no.

How do you respond when a family member or friend does not seem to understand that you are going to keep saying no, no matter how many times they ask?

Say no. No comment.

Don't actually say the words "no comment." You just say no. No commentary needed. Don't try to explain over and over. You might have to say no a dozen or a hundred more times.

Some people just need to hear you say no.

27

NO, THANK YOU

There are many ways to say no.

I am sure you will come up with more as you learn to embrace this small but beautiful word. Can I make one more suggestion? No matter what no you decide to use, you can always be polite.

Learn to say, "No, thank you"!

NO CONCLUSION

NO REMINDERS

- There are many ways to say no. Far more than are written in this section. All of them can be beautiful when used in the appropriate situation.
- You can make up your own nos to add to your personal menu.
- You should experiment and try many different nos to learn which ones fit you best.
- The only way to get good at saying no is to practice, so get started.
- Some nos have a price. Remember, if you say yes when you should say no, the cost is always greater!
- Not every no works in every situation and with every person. Experiment, practice, pay attention to how people respond, and as time passes, you will get better at saying no.
- You can always be courteous and polite when you say no.

NO EXERCISE

Experiment with five new nos you learned while reading this section of the book. Look for opportunities to say no, be intentional in how you word your no, and have fun—you are learning to say no in five new and exciting ways! Watch how people respond. Take note of how effectively each no works. Remember, some of these take practice to perfect. Don't worry, you will have a lot of opportunities to say no.

◆ ——————————————————————————————— ◆

You might want to identify or make up three fresh new ways to say no that were not discussed in this section of the book. If you do, please feel free to share them with me. If you drop me a note at my website *(www. kevingharney.com)*, I will make a point of sharing your wisdom with others. If you don't want to share your ideas with me, just say no. I won't feel bad.

PICKING YOUR

NOS

I couldn't resist.

The title of this section may be lighthearted, but the content is quite serious. The idea is simple. Once you have developed a great menu of nos, you need to be wise in deciding which no is right for each of life's situations. Only you can pick your nos.

No one can decide for you. But I want to encourage you. In time, you will get better at making these decisions! Yoda would put it this way: "Decide you must. Decide you will. Master of the no you shall become!"

28

SPARE YOUR NOS

⁂

Years ago, when our sons were just little guys, my wife was reading a parenting book. Sherry is both an educator and theologian by formal education and a lifelong student by choice. She is always reading a couple of books, and I am the recipient of her frequent insights from an array of authors, spanning the centuries.

She shared this nugget with me: "This author says that parents should spare their nos and save them for the times when they really matter."⁶ That made sense to me. We talked about it and how we might apply that principle to our parenting.

I can remember a day when this was tested. Our sons slept in beds that had frames, box springs, and mattresses. They all had nice little sleeping suits with matching pants and shirts (commonly called pajamas). But then one of our boys questioned this setup. He asked if he could get rid of the bed frame and box spring. He wanted his mattress on the floor. And he also wanted to be free to stop wearing his matching pajamas.

This was hard for Sherry, but we agreed to spare our no in this instance and say yes. There was no good reason to say no.

So our son made the shift, and soon all three of the boys were sleeping on a mattress on the floor.

There were many times when we had to say no to our sons. We decided not to waste our nos on trivial things like the style of their bed or the outfit they wore at night.

When you pick your nos, always ask the question, "Do I really need to say no to this?" Spare your nos.

29

NO CONTEXT

⟶※⟵

As you pick your nos, always consider the context. "Where am I? Who am I talking to? Why are they asking me this question?" Your context will help you determine which no is best and most winsome. Your context might even lead you to say a gracious yes.

If a stranger on the street confronts me harshly and tries to pressure me into giving them cash on the spot, saying no is easy. But if I encounter a person who is genuinely hurting and humble and seems to be sincere in their need, my response will be quite different.

If I land at an airport and a stranger offers me a ride and reaches out to pick up my bags without my permission, he will get a quick, harsh, and definitive no! I have been in this situation many times, and a firm and loud no is the only way to resist an aggressive taxi driver.

If a little girl in my neighborhood knocks on the door and asks if I would like to buy some Girl Scout cookies, I will respond very differently. If I shout no at her, I will terrify this sweet young girl and leave her in tears.

But if I have already bought cookies from two Girl Scouts (which is my limit; I love Thin Mints chilled in the fridge), I *am* going to tell her no. I will do it kindly. I will explain why. And I will encourage her to come to our house earlier next year (and be sure to bring plenty of Thin Mints). But I will tell her no.

The type of no you use should always be determined by the context.

30

SCARY NOS

———✦———

Several years ago, a publisher hired my wife to do a major project. They asked her to research, select, and edit more than three hundred daily readings for a devotional Bible designed for older and more mature people. This would be the biggest project of her freelance publishing career. She was excited to dig in.

When the contracts were drawn up and the timetable was finalized, there was one big challenge. The publication schedule required her to begin working at the start of the summer if she hoped to hit her deadline. She would need to put in twenty to thirty hours a week, every week of the summer.

Sherry evaluated all the variables. If she had been asked to begin writing during the school year, it would have been manageable. She knew what it would take to do this project with excellence, and she realized that during the summer, she could not give it the attention needed and be a full-time mother to our three boys.

Our sons were seven, five, and three at the time. Behind our back yard was a pond of open water. Our youngest son could not swim. Our middle son was just learning.

She spent a week trying to navigate the project and care for our sons. There were times when she had to let them out of the house to enjoy the beautiful Michigan summer, and Sherry saw that there was no way she could care for our boys and do the project. There was tension between her passion to be an engaged mom and her desire to do this project. But she did not want to hurt her relationship with the publisher or pass up the additional income this project would provide.

Sherry called the publisher and said, "I am so sorry. I have realized that I can't do this project and hit the deadline. I have three boys, and they need to play outside, and I need to be free to spend time with them through the summer. I simply can't balance being a caring mom and doing my best work for you on this project. I have to say no."

My wife did not give a simple no. She explained that she really wanted to do the project. She was excited about it. But the timing did not work.

Her editor's response was a complete surprise.

"That's one of the things we love about you! You know your priorities and stick to them!" The publisher came back with a counteroffer: "What if we hired you an assistant to do the data entry, the coding of the manuscript, and some of the research? Then you could start at the end of summer and still hit your deadline."

Sherry was thrilled and humbled. She said yes and enjoyed the summer with the boys and then was able to complete the manuscript on time. To this day, it remains one of her favorite projects.[7]

It was a scary no. Sherry thought she would lose the contract and possibly some future writing opportunities.

In the end, she was affirmed and was able to work out a schedule that enabled her to balance both commitments.

When you face a scary no, be honest and clear and give reasons for your no. Not every no will work out like this one did for my wife, but sometimes it will. You just have to take that chance and be willing to live with the outcome.

31

HARD NOS

S ometimes a no can be hard because it requires you to speak a challenging truth, something another person may not want to hear.

Sherry and I were asked to consider a major project in partnership with a well-known pastor, an international ministry, and a major publisher. We were both honored and agreed to meet to discuss the proposal.

We met with two leaders. One was the head of the large ministry that would be providing the content. The other was the publisher's lead editor.

As we had lunch and talked, it became clear that we would be creating about 60 percent to 70 percent of the content in these studies. About 30 percent to 40 percent would be gleaned from existing materials written by someone else. Near the end of the lunch, we were asked, "Would it be okay if your names were not on these studies, and if you did not receive any of the royalties?"

I paused to ponder the question. I had heard of ghostwriters, but I had never been asked to be one. The idea did not sit well with me. I considered my words and picked my no carefully.

I pondered the question, "Would it be okay if your names were not on the studies?"

I spoke clearly and calmly. "No, I believe that is immoral!"

I could tell the editor was a little shocked and hurt. We had worked together on a number of projects, and I considered him a friend. He knew me well enough to know that I can be blunt. He was clearly not ready for my response.

He said, "It is a fairly common practice in publishing."

I replied, "I did not say it was uncommon. I said I believe it is immoral!"

I pointed out that if a college student turned in a paper that was 60 percent to 70 percent someone else's work, they would be disciplined and possibly thrown out of school. Claiming someone else's work as your own is called plagiarism. So I said it again. "It is immoral."

At that moment, I needed a direct and uncompromising no, a nuclear no!

To our surprise, they hired us, considered our concerns, and put our names on each of the studies.

Sometimes a hard no is exactly what you need to make a point.

Is there a hard no you have been avoiding? What are the moments in your life when you need to be prepared with a hard no? Commit yourself to speak hard nos with clarity, strength, and humility. You will be glad you did!

32

DANGEROUS NOS

·※·

Some circumstances call for a no that is risky. We speak this kind of no when we believe we hold the moral high ground or believe we have no other option. We count the cost and say no.

I remember it like it was yesterday, though it was close to fifty years ago. My dad was driving down a busy highway with my mom beside him in the front seat of our station wagon. Two of my siblings and I were lying down in the back of the car.

It was about two decades before the law mandated that passengers wear seat belts, but there were speed limits posted along the road. My dad saw the flashing light and heard the siren coming from the police car behind him, but instead of pulling over, he continued driving, slightly slower. When he reached the next off-ramp, he pulled off the highway and onto the side of a safe and traffic-free road.

The officer came to his window, and he was angry! He ordered my dad to get out of the car and lectured him for several minutes about the requirement to pull directly over when a police officer sounds a siren and flashes their lights. We could all hear the conversation and feel the intensity of the officer.

My dad listened. And then he responded with logic and clarity, articulating that he had three young children and a wife with him, and he would not park on the side of a busy highway with his family in the car.

The officer disagreed. "The next time you hear a siren and see the lights, you will pull over immediately!"

But my dad held his ground. "No, I will not! I will find the first available place I deem safe, and then I will pull over."

I won't include the full-color commentary of their debate. But that day, my dad taught me an important lesson as I watched him interact with the officer. There are times when you must speak a dangerous no! He could have been arrested. He took a risk.

A dangerous no might cost you. But there are times when you must stand your ground and count the cost for the sake of something—or someone—you value and love. It is worth the risk.

Is there a dangerous no you have been avoiding or pushing to the back burner? Do you need to consider the consequences and still speak this no?

NO GENTLENESS

When you are confident you need to say no and are looking at your menu of nos, wanting to make a wise choice, ask yourself this question: "What is the most gentle no I can speak and still accomplish my desired results?"

Saying no can seem harsh in and of itself.

So always seek to use the least force necessary.

34

NO TO THE NO MONSTER

When I was a little boy, I believed a monster lived under my bed. Whenever I needed to go to the bathroom during the night, I would leap from the edge of my bed to avoid his hairy arms just waiting to grab my legs. As I grew older, I learned that monsters are not real.

Then, as I grew even older, I learned that some monsters are very real.

There is a type of person I call the No Monster. Their response to any and every question you ask is always, perpetually no. Saying no is their default option for every situation.

Because I've written this book encouraging you to treat no as a beautiful, helpful, life-changing word, you might assume I am a fan of the No Monster. I am not. There are times when we must wisely say no, and there are times when we must enthusiastically say yes. But we should not say no automatically to everything.

The No Monster is the parent who says no to every question their child asks until she no longer bothers asking. The No Monster is the boss who believes that the only way to motivate is through control, so he says no to every new idea. The No Monster is the teacher who refuses to adapt and give space for kids to be kids, enforcing a harsh discipline that kills creativity and quenches a love for learning. There are No Monsters all around us.

Again, I want to emphasize the beauty of saying no. For most of you, saying yes is easy; the challenge is in asserting yourself and giving a firm no. But I want to warn you against allowing the pendulum to swing the other way. If you become a No Monster, you will miss out on countless wonderful human interactions.

So how do you avoid overusing your no?

I have a friend named Ben. He and his wife, Loretta, have raised a wonderful family with three sons and one daughter, and they have been an example to me and my wife on many levels. They are parents who know how to set healthy boundaries, and they wisely say no to their children, but they are the farthest thing from No Monsters.

Ben once told me of a time when one of his sons came to him, asking if he could sleep on the floor. A No Monster would have considered the problems and obstacles.

- "No, you have a perfectly good bed."
- "No, the floor is dirty."
- "No, you will get a backache."

Instead Ben asked his son a simple question. "Why do you want to sleep on the floor?"

His son explained that in Sunday school that week, his teacher had taught them about the Roman soldiers and how they had lived in the days of Jesus. He had learned that soldiers slept on the ground so they were ready for whatever assignment they were given and always prepared for battle. The young boy thought this was cool. He wanted to try it for himself, and so he was asking his father for permission.

As you might have guessed, Ben gave him permission to sleep on the floor to see how he liked it. A few days later, his son was back in his bed. Apparently, he had decided there were no major battles he needed to prepare for.

Consider what would have happened if Ben had responded as a No Monster. He would have missed out on a great conversation with his son, and his son would have missed out on the chance to test what he had learned about Roman soldiers.

Look closely at your response patterns. By all means, learn to say no and discern the right no for the right time. But don't become a No Monster. No is a beautiful word when it is used wisely, but if we respond negatively to every conversation, question, or idea that comes along, we must change our ways.

35

STRATEGIC NOS

For many years, I was a generalist. As a pastor and author, I was invited to speak at conferences and events. My wife and I would travel and speak on topics ranging from marriage to leadership to outreach, as well as a host of other subjects.

I enjoyed presenting talks in a wide variety of settings, on diverse subjects, to a broad range of people. I felt honored that people wanted to have me speak to their constituents.

As my plate filled up, I had to be strategic in my choices. I looked at the topics people were asking me to talk about. I considered my own interests and asked myself, "What are the topics I'm most passionate about, the things I couldn't stop talking about even if I tried?" I realized there were two things that fit this category—leadership and outreach.

Now, there are only two topics I'll travel to speak about: how to reach out to others with the love of Jesus in a way that is natural and organic, and how to lead in a way that is effective and healthy. This does not mean I have nothing to say on other topics. But I choose to limit myself to what I feel most passionate about, focusing on the topics that are closest to my heart.

Other subjects might be important to other people, but they are not where I will invest my limited time and energy.

Here is why this is so beautiful. By focusing on what I am most excited and passionate about, I free myself to say no to invitations. These may be good opportunities to speak to lovely people, but if I were to say yes, it would crowd out the opportunities to speak on the topics I love most. I no longer have to ponder, struggle, or deliberate, because I have done the hard work of asking myself, "What will my life be about? Where will I focus my energy? To what will I devote myself?"

Take time to answer these three questions. Once you know the answer, commit to saying no to opportunities that don't align with the unique gifts, passions, and talents God has given you. When you learn to say yes to what you love most, almost everything else is an easy no.

In the next section, we will dig into a series of strategic ideas that will help you know when to say no and when to say yes.

NO CONCLUSION

NO REMINDERS

- Knowing your nos is just the start. You need to choose the right no for each situation.
- Be frugal with your nos so when you use them, they mean something.
- Not all nos are effective in all situations and with all people. Learn to discern your context so you can pick your nos wisely.
- Sometimes saying no is scary, dangerous, and just plain hard. Have the courage to still say no.
- Look in the mirror. Listen to yourself. If you have become a No Monster, it is time to use your nos more sparingly.

NO EXERCISE

Identify one situation you are facing right now in which you are going to have to say no. Write down three possible ways you can do that. Use the nos in section 2 or come up with your own ideas. Then describe the situation and your three possible nos to a trusted friend. Ask for their insight. Finally, pick your no and give it a try. Be sure you are as gentle as possible while being crystal clear.

If you know someone who is a No Monster, watch and listen to them for a month. Study their patterns. Decide not to be like them when it comes to how often and how automatically they say no. If you have a safe relationship, invite them to read chapter 34.

PART

4

NO

STRATEGY

Most good things that happen in life are planned and deliberate, the result of thoughtful choices and hard work. While there are occasions when wonderful things apparently just come to pass, these occurrences are the outliers, not the norm. And when good things *seem* to happen randomly, there is often someone behind the scenes, steadily and stealthily working out a strategy, and you are reaping the benefits.

In this section, we will learn that saying no is a strategic learning process. If you want to discover the beauty and freedom that comes when you say no, you will have to develop a series of deliberate and tactical strategies.

Let's get started.

36

NO WITH A SMILE

Strategy number one: no matter which no you use and no matter how firm you might have to be, try to say no with a smile.

Studies show that when we smile, our physical and emotional condition changes for the better. Our body releases feel-good chemicals including dopamine, endorphins, and serotonin. In addition, our smile impacts others in very positive ways and can change their emotional condition for the better.[8]

A little sugar almost always makes the medicine go down easier, and a smile can make hearing no a positive experience.

37

NO MARGIN

I think I need to cut back on some of my classes."

My son was away at college, and we were talking on the phone. He was feeling overwhelmed, with far too much on his plate.

I asked him why he was feeling this way. He explained that between being an RA (resident assistant), serving as a professor's teaching assistant, and working in the registrar's office, he had no spare time. He was holding down three part-time jobs and taking a full academic load, all while trying to maintain a meaningful social life with his friends.

The picture was coming into focus.

For the first time in his young adult life, my son had hit his margin. He'd pushed too far. He was learning that he had only so many hours in a week and a limited reserve of energy to accomplish all he wanted to do.

I explained that he was at a good point in his development, facing the reality of his limitations. He was learning about the need to say no. We talked about the value of knowing our margin. He saw the need to learn how to take some things off his plate so he could focus on what was most important.

I pointed out some of the signals that can appear in our life, like a red light on the dashboard of a car that warns us that the engine is overheating and about to shut down. One way to identify these signals is to ask specific questions.

- "Am I losing my sense of peace?" If you say yes, it is a red light.
- "Do I see my pace as unsustainable over time?" A yes is a warning.
- "Is my health suffering and my energy level dropping?" Answer yes and you have a problem.
- "Are the people around me expressing concern about my pace or the load I am carrying?" I should pay attention.

Some people learn this lesson later in life, after years of burning out and feeling stretched too thin. Some never learn. I was delighted to see my son discovering his limits at a relatively young age.

My son began to examine his life, prioritizing what mattered most and then saying no to a number of things that were not as important. Within a few weeks, his life began improving as he regained control of his time.

Peace increased, pace slowed (to normal busy), health returned, and the people in his life (including his dad and mom) no longer worried about him.

Do you know your No Margin? This is the point where you sense you are stretched thin and have taken on too much. You've said yes to far too many things. What do you do when you reach your No Margin?

Start by identifying your personal limitations. Ask the four preceding questions. Make an honest assessment of your energy level (because this varies from person to person). Consider your current season of life. Think about your short-term and long-term priorities. And begin to set appropriate boundaries.

When you realize you have hit your No Margin, you need to learn to say no more aggressively. Take some things off your plate. In these seasons of life, you are wise to refrain from any new yeses until you have said some tactical nos.

38

TELLING ME NO

The one person I don't like to say no to is myself. I want ice cream at ten o'clock at night. Since I am an adult, the only person who can tell me no is me! I must learn to have self control.

I often want to hit the snooze button on my alarm and sleep in rather than getting out of bed and exercising before I go to work.

I need to tell me and the snooze button no.

When I start feeling selfish and want my way, who will tell me no? You know the answer to that question!

I was a new pastor at a small country church in Michigan. They had used the same music in their Sunday services for a hundred years. Innovating and trying new things was not part of the culture. I decided to move the church out of the 70s (and by that, I mean the 1770s), so we introduced some more-modern songs and began using the guitar rather than the organ on some of the songs.

The next morning, I got a call from an elderly woman at the church. She wanted to come by the office and talk with me. I had been a pastor long enough to know that a Monday morning call and a request for a face-to-face meeting was almost never good. I was certain she was unhappy about something I had done or said.

We sat in my office, and she explained that she did not like the new music. "I like the old hymns, I prefer the organ, and this new music does not make me feel close to God. And I don't like the guitar." I tried not to take it personally, though I was the one playing the guitar on the new songs just twenty-four hours earlier.

I could see she was trying to be kind but also very honest. I could also sense she was hurting. She was afraid of losing something she loved, a style of music that stirred her soul.

I decided not to defend the music or myself. Instead I asked her a question. "Do you think we should stop trying new music with new instrumental arrangements?"

She paused. I could tell she was thinking about her response. Her next words shocked me. "No, I think we *should* do the new music! I think we *should* use the guitar. I think the young people will like it, and maybe new people who come to the church will enjoy it. I just wanted you to know that I don't like it!"

I sat there quietly for a few moments, trying to process what she had just said. This woman was telling me,

- "I will say no to what I love, for the sake of others."
- "I will say no to me so I can say yes to the needs of people who are different from me."
- "I will sacrifice for a greater good."

I almost wept.

I understood now that she wanted her pastor to know this was hard for her. It was costing her something. But she was ready to say no to her wants, needs, and desires for the sake of others.

Since that Monday morning conversation thirty years ago, that woman has been one of my heroes. That day, she taught me that one of the most courageous things I can do is say no to *me*!

Learn how to say no to yourself. And not just for your own sake. Learn how to say no for the sake of others. It will not be easy. But this is what makes life meaningful, as we give up what we want in order to love others. Love turns a difficult no—a no to me—into a beautiful word.

What is a no you need to say to yourself but have been avoiding? How will saying no help you? How will it positively impact others? What is keeping you from saying no, and how can you remove this obstacle? Have the courage to look in the mirror and say no!

39

TELLING YOU NO

I dedicated this book to my father, Terry Harney. My father said no to me more times than anyone else in my life. I can still hear his strong voice declaring, "That is not acceptable behavior in this household."

In our home, there were certain attitudes, ways of speaking, and activities that were not allowed.

Ever.

And if you adopted or engaged in one of them, it evoked a firm and consistent no, expressed in a variety of articulate and memorable ways.

When I was younger, I did not fully appreciate the clear boundaries my dad provided for me. Later in life, I began to see that having someone tell me no through my childhood and teenage years was a gift and a blessing. My father and mother said no to me, not because they wanted to control my life but because they loved me and wanted the best for me.

They did not want me growing up to be selfish, petty, or lazy. They were teaching me the beauty of a life lived with self-restraint, boundaries, and balance. I do not know who I would be or what I would be doing today if my parents had failed to tell me no.

As I was raising my children, I wanted them to understand that I loved them by setting boundaries and saying no when it was the right thing to do. I still remember the first time I responded to one of my sons with a booming, "That is not acceptable behavior in this household." As soon as the words had passed my lips, I felt an urge to look over my shoulder to see whether my father had walked into the room. The tone and cadence of my words sounded just like him.

Over the years, this phrase—a clear indication of what is a yes and what is a no—became a mantra in our household. I said it when our boys crossed a line or acted inappropriately. And it was effective, because my boys understood that this was one way I was showing my love for them, making it clear that no, you will not become that kind of person.

Today all three of my sons are married, and I have a hunch that someday their children will hear a clear and resounding, "That is not acceptable behavior in this household." My sons know that if they want to love their children well, they will pass on a legacy of telling them no.

This week, think about the people you love, those closest to you. Are there behaviors, attitudes, and activities that need a firm no? Look for ways of saying no to the ones you love most, knowing that if you fail to do this, you are failing to love them well.

And if you have kids, feel free to borrow my dad's line if it feels appropriate in your setting. Try saying, "That is not acceptable behavior in this household."

40

NO MORE

⁂

"No more, please!"

Though I love a good meal, there are times when I've been a guest at dinner and had to refuse a second or third helping. I've eaten my fill and can't fit in another bite! Or I know I should not.

There are times when we must say no, not because we do not enjoy something or cannot be involved but because there is the risk of *excess*, of doing too much. This no is about having the wisdom to know when agreeing to or continuing to do something would be counterproductive, unnecessary, or inordinate. When you identify these situations, you can wisely and preemptively declare, "No more!"

In these moments, it is always necessary to speak these words to yourself.

Often, we will also need to speak them to other people as well.

I began attending school when I was four years old, and I continued formal studies through high school, college, and graduate school, earning a master's degree and a doctorate. Through several of those years, I worked to pay for my studies and to put food on the table. My doctoral work was exactly what I needed to advance my learning, and it drove me to pursue new opportunities. When I finished my degree, I said to my wife (and to myself), "No more formal education."

Since that time, I have had many people encourage me to consider an additional doctorate, one that would open the door for me to teach in an academy. These encouragements tend to come from people who live and work in academic settings and feel a PhD is the pinnacle of education—the key that opens all other doors. Every time someone tries to sell me on this idea, I gently let him or her know that I've decided to conclude my formal education. I've said, "No more," and I'm sticking with that no!

Still, no matter how clear I am, some people keep pushing me. They try to build a case for why they think I should change course and go back to school. I explain that I've not stopped learning and am always engaged in a self-designed study program, one that has no tuition and is focused on the topics I need.

Some of these friends may never understand why I refuse their advice. But there are times when I must say, "No more," and stick to it. I know it is the right decision for me, and I don't have to think twice about it. It's an automatic no.

We have one life to live, and we can't do it all. When you say yes to something, you are saying no to something else. You are the one responsible for saying, "No more," for your life.

Are there things you are doing that are no longer necessary? Are you feeling pressure from someone you respect and care about, but you know that what they want you to do is not something you need in your life? Have you maxed out in a specific area, but you just keeping taking on more and more?

Identify your No More situations. Declare them. Stick to them. Say, "No more!"

41

NO STALLING

⟶✦⟵

My buddy Ron called and asked me a simple question.

"Hey, Kevin, do you want to go golfing with me and some of my friends for a few days?"

He shared the details. Ron was treating everyone, paying the costs for the entire trip. We would be traveling on a private plane to a world-class golf course called Sand Hills in Nebraska.

Unfortunately, the dates he gave were problematic. I had a few other commitments already on my schedule. I paused, disappointed, and let him know I couldn't make it.

"No. Sadly, those dates won't work for me. But thanks for the offer."

Ron was fine about it. We chatted briefly and the phone call ended.

I couldn't get his invitation out of my head. Fifteen minutes passed, and I took a closer look at my schedule and saw that I could probably make a couple of calls, shift a few things around, and join the guys. I knew this was a trip I could not afford if I was paying.

It was a once-in-a-lifetime opportunity.

I called Ron back and asked, "Hey, is the offer still open?"

His response was quick and matter-of-fact. "Sorry, I already filled your spot!"

At first, I thought he was joking. It had been only fifteen minutes. "Seriously, I can make it work."

"Seriously, your spot is gone. I already called the next guy on my list."

I was disappointed, but I fully understood.

Sometime later, Ron and I were having lunch.

"Can I give you some advice?" he asked.

I said, "Yes."

"Do you remember our conversation the other day, when I offered to take you and some guys on a golf trip to Nebraska?"

I assured him that I did remember.

"Next time I invite you to do something like that, just say yes." He went on to explain, "After you tell me yes, go to work on the details, and if it turns out you can't make it, just call me back and cancel. You can always tell me no later, when you've had time to try to make it work."

I now call this No Stalling. Whenever I think I may have to say no, but I'm not 100 percent sure, I am comfortable giving a yes or a maybe, a response that allows me some additional time to figure out if I can make it work. That way I don't close the door.

Let me offer a few warnings if you decide to use this delayed no. First, try to get a clear sense of the cost for the person asking you. If a delay will be a huge inconvenience for them, you may need to be more decisive in your response. In addition, this is a no you will want to use sparingly. If you say yes to everything, only to pull out on those commitments later, you will undermine your credibility.

With these cautions in mind, I am comfortable giving a delayed no if necessary.

If you think there is a good possibility you might be able to manage a yes, and you really want to say yes, don't declare a premature no.

For a year after this conversation with my friend Ron, I jokingly answered every phone call from him with these words: "Yes! I'm in! The answer is yes."

If you think you can say yes, but you need more time, it's okay to stall a bit before giving a definitive no. Keep your options open and say no later if you must.

42

NO GUTS

Have you ever been given an invitation, an offer, or an opportunity that seems attractive, but something deep inside you screams, *Say no!*? You can't explain why. You don't have any clear evidence that trouble is afoot. Yet the red light is flashing in the back of your mind. An alarm is going off. Everything in your gut is saying, *Beware!*

Pay attention to that voice. Listen. Dare to follow your gut and say no! Often our gut instinct is telling us something our conscious mind has not yet perceived or understood. There is a good chance you could end up regretting saying yes in these situations.

Malcolm Gladwell is a brilliant, humble writer. He is an excellent researcher, and I love reading his books and articles. In the book *Blink*, Gladwell writes about our ability to "know" something without knowing, to "think" without consciously thinking.[9] Gladwell points to the wisdom of trusting that intangible thing inside us that can access a level of understanding beyond our conscious thought process. "Gut" refers to our innate ability to process multiple sensory inputs beyond what we see and hear at a surface level. His point is that there are times when we have no obvious way of knowing why we know something, but we are sure we do.

Don't ignore your gut. It may know something you don't. And if something inside you is screaming no, have the guts to listen.

43

AUTOMATIC NOS

I've hinted at the power of setting priorities, but I'd like to take that one step farther. How do you empower your priorities in your day-to-day decisions? Here is a simple and clear habit you can develop to make sure you are doing the things you most want to do.

If you know what matters most to you, don't stop there. Make a list of your automatic nos. These are the things you will not do, no matter what, and that will not change; you will always say no. This can cover a wide range of life experiences.

Determine in advance that you will say no to these things. You would be wise to pick one or two nos you feel would be most helpful in these situations and practice them until the response becomes automatic. Once you have these responses locked in your mind, commit to answer quickly and confidently every time one of these situations presents itself. Here are some examples from my life, a few of my automatic nos.

- *"Do you want to go out for a beer?"* "No, but I would love to get a root beer or a sparkling fruit juice and hang out."

(For the record, I am a bit of a root beer aficionado.) If you have read all the chapters in this book up to this point, you know my family history with alcoholism.

- *"Would you like a dessert menu?"* "No, thanks!" If they try to hand it to me, I don't take it. I just smile and decline. I know that if I take the menu, all hope is lost, especially if they have something that includes chocolate and vanilla ice cream.

- *"Have you ever tried [you name the recreational drug], and would you be interested?"* "No, and you don't ever have to ask me that kind of question again."

- *"Can I tell you about a problem I have with someone else?"* "No, unless you have tried to resolve the issue with them and they refused. If you have tried to reconcile and they were not responsive, you can talk with me about it. But you must be fully committed to going with me to that person because you are seeking to heal the relationship. If that is not the plan, then no, you can't tell me about them. That is gossip and does not help you, them, me, or anyone." (By the way, I got the basic structure of this response from Jesus. See Matthew 18:15–16.)

This is just a short list of some of the automatic nos I have loaded in my mind and heart.

44

NO APOLOGIES

When you begin saying no, some people won't understand. They will push back, and in their own way they will try to get you to say yes to whatever they want or need. They have become accustomed to your being a Yes Machine, and they will not know how to respond to your newfound commitment to saying no.

To help you deal with this, I offer you a strategy I call No Apology.

Get this firmly in your mind: "I have *nothing* to apologize for when I say no." In saying no, you are simply establishing healthy boundaries. You have decided that others will not rule your life and that the most important things must come first. You know there will be a cost and that there will be some things you will no longer have time or energy to do. This is how healthy, mature people live.

It's normal and good.

None of this requires an apology. So don't give one! No apologies.

There will be people you love and care about who will have a hard time with your firm conviction and your consistent nos.

They may be confused at first, since you once did whatever they wanted. Now you are saying no regularly, and they might even interpret this as a lack of love and care. They may even accuse you of being selfish. What can you say that will help them feel a little better and begin navigating this new world you are building?

Here are a few No Apologies. These are not ways to apologize. You are not saying you are sorry for living a healthier life or making wise choices. You are not expressing any regret for saying no. Each of these is a response of empathy, a way of indicating that you understand how your healthy choices might be hard for them.

- "I'm sorry this does not make sense to you. Can I try to explain why I am establishing clear boundaries and saying no more often?"
- "I'm sorry my choices don't line up with what you want. I can see this is hard for you, and that is not my intention."
- "I'm sorry you feel my decision to say no has changed our relationship. I think we can work through this, but you need to know that I will continue to keep the boundaries I am setting for my life."
- "I'm sorry you feel hurt by my saying no. I really care about you, and it is not my goal to cause you pain."

These responses reinforce your commitment to say no and are an effort to extend grace to people and acknowledge that you understand how your choices might adversely impact their life, making them uncomfortable or frustrated.

If you have a close relationship with the person and want to help them grow a healthier life, you might consider walking them through the content of this book, sharing with them what you are learning. Help them discover for themselves the beauty of no.

45

NO HONESTY

A t this point in the book, we're moving from the basics to
some of the advanced strategies. Congratulations! You've
come a long way.

We live in a world where, unfortunately, it is rare to hear
someone speaking truth with a thoughtful and gracious spirit.
Many people have a hard time telling someone no and explaining why in a respectful and loving manner. Human beings are
masters at self-deception, and we have a difficult time facing
our own frailties and mistakes.

I came face-to-face with my capacity for self-deception on
a family vacation several years ago. At the time, our sons were
still quite young, and I had brought some work with me (already
a bad sign). One night, I was working and I read an insight from
a leader I respect. He was talking about his work and how it
demanded lots of late nights at the office. To protect his family,
he had established a rule of working late no more than three
nights a week. He made a commitment to be home four nights
each week with his family.

I appreciated the clarity of his rule, especially because I was driving myself hard and knew I was starting to overextend.

I mentioned to my wife what I had just read. I told her, "If I'm not careful, I could end up back at the office every night of the week!"

She looked at me with firm kindness. "Kevin, you *do* go back to the office every night of the week."

I responded with profound maturity. "I do not!"

She gently insisted. "I think you do."

I was determined to prove her wrong. I got up and walked to the other room to grab my calendar. As I sat there, reviewing my schedule, something inside me broke. I looked back one week, then two weeks, then three. I had to go back an entire month before I found a single night when I had gone home on time and stayed home the whole night. I hadn't realized how out of control my life had become. But my family had noticed.

I had sworn I would never be *that* husband.

I had told myself I would not be the dad who let his work rule his life.

I had a perception of myself that was neither honest nor accurate. My wife had the real picture. I had declared how I saw reality, but she said with piercing honesty, "No, that is not how things are."

At that moment, I faced a choice. I could continue living in the darkness of my self-deception. Or I could step into the light, hear the truth, and say no to the absurd and destructive lifestyle I was creating.

By the grace of God, I chose the second option. I apologized to my wife and to my sons. I promised to say no to the flood of demands and the never-ending expectations of hundreds of well-meaning people who wanted my time. I also apologized to my church board and the congregation the following Sunday, and I confessed that my life had spun out of control. I admitted that my work was consuming me, and I told them I needed to make some serious changes, say some bold nos, set some healthy boundaries, and begin living a more balanced life.

To my surprise and delight, the board members and the congregation all encouraged me to make more time for my family. I limited myself to three—and in rare situations, four—nights of work a week. I committed to taking one full day off each week, and I disciplined myself not to check in with the office on my day off. It wasn't easy! I had to say a lot of nos.

To help me make the transition out of my overcommitted lifestyle, my wife asked me to write down, at the start of each week, what nights I would be staying home. Then she posted these dates on a big calendar hanging on the wall in the entryway to our house from the garage. As they went in and out, all three of our boys would see the words boldly printed: "DAD HOME NIGHT."

I stuck to this practice tenaciously. The first night I came home for a Dad Home Night, my youngest son was standing on the washing machine near the entryway. He jumped on my back as I walked in. "It's a Dad Home Night!" he declared. All three boys were at the house, and we had a great evening together. For the next three weeks, every night I walked in the door on a Dad Home Night, my son "surprised" me by jumping on my back. It quickly became a ritual for us.

When the fourth week came, I entered the house and was shocked when no one was there to jump on my back. I called for my youngest son. No response. I called the other two boys. Nothing.

I found my wife and asked her where the boys were. She explained that all three were off playing with friends.

"Didn't you tell the boys it was a Dad Home Night?" I asked.

"Yes, I told them," she said, "but they all said, 'Dad is always here!'"

That was the best thing she could have told me.

I am thankful that my wife had the strength and integrity to speak an honest no to me.

Are there deep and honest nos you need to speak to people you love? Are you ready and willing to hear honest nos that peel back self-deception and reveal the way things really are? If so, deep healing can happen in your life and relationships.

46

YOUR NOS WILL
DEFINE YOUR LIFE

Most of us think our life is defined by what we do. We focus on the things we say yes to. We choose the people, activities, and experiences that will shape our character, our destiny, and our legacy.

To some extent, it's true—our yeses have a big impact on our life.

I believe our nos are just as powerful and life-changing. In some cases, they are even more important than a strategic yes.

How so?

People today can choose all sorts of good things to do. The challenge is not in saying yes but in saying yes to only the most significant things. And that means saying no to many other things.

Learning to say no protects you from being consumed by the less important things of life. When you come to the end of your life, you will look back and discover that it has been your nos that have defined who you have become.

NO CONCLUSION

NO REMINDERS

- Nothing valuable happens by chance. To accomplish great things, you need to be strategic and diligent in your approach, and this includes saying no.
- You have a limited amount of time, energy, and emotional capital. Study yourself and make sure you don't exceed your margin. To do this, you will need to say some strategic nos.
- The first person you must say no to is yourself. This means you must be ready to count the cost and make sacrifices.
- Saying no to the people in your life is one of the greatest expressions of love and care.
- Sometimes a delayed no is what you need, at least for now.
- Some nos should be automatic and unchanging. Identify these and be ready to say no before the situation presents itself.
- Learning to say no will demand the kind of honesty that will stretch you, but it will be worth it!

NO EXERCISE

I shared my list of automatic nos. Take time to make your list of three to five situations in which you should be ready to say no with tenacious consistency. Once you identify the situations, pick one or two specific nos that you will be ready to speak when you face these circumstances. Practice saying these nos so you are prepared when the moment comes, because it will.

PART

5

CRITICAL

NOS

Some nos are minor. Their consequences are hardly noticed.

Other nos are quite important and need to be spoken with firm conviction and clarity.

Then there are critical nos. These are the nos that define your life, protect what matters most, and launch you into the heights of meaning and joy.

47

NO MORALITY

A moral and virtuous life requires many nos. One of the most well-known and best examples of this is found in the Old Testament of the Bible. In both Exodus 20 and Deuteronomy 5, we find God giving his people a series of commandments. Ten of them, in fact.

For the most part, these ten big commands are expressed in terms of what should *not* be done. They could have been phrased in positive terms, but a heavenly no is often exactly what hard-of-hearing people like you and me need.

Here are the ten big rules God gave his people. In some versions, you may have heard the no as a "Thou Shalt Not." It's still a no.

1. No other gods.
2. No making images to worship.
3. No misuse of God's name.
4. Remember the Sabbath day (no work on this day).
5. Honor your father and mother (no disrespect).
6. No murder.

7. No adultery.
8. No stealing.
9. No false witnessing.
10. No coveting (wanting and lusting over) what belongs to others.

Altogether there are eight nos, one remember, and one honor. Why did God give these rules? The Bible tells us that it was so God's people would thrive and experience his blessings. God loves his children and wants the best for us. Like any good parent, he gives rules and guidelines to keep the kids on the right path. A parent who stands silently watching their child run off a cliff or reach into a fire is unloving and irresponsible.

Many today laugh at the idea of moral absolutes or norms that are always true for all people. They don't believe there is a right way, a healthy way, we were designed to live. But this is a relatively recent way of thinking. For thousands of years, it has been understood that when people follow certain rules, human life thrives and prospers. God cares about you enough to tell you the truth. He doesn't want to see you run off the cliff, so he puts guardrails on the path of your life. And he does this as an act of love.

A divine no is one of the most beautiful words you will ever hear. Pay attention to it. Learn God's wisdom, and you will discover the freedom, joy, and safety of following God's nos.

One day, you may even learn to love God's nos.

48

NO TEMPTATION

An epic battle is portrayed in the pages of the Bible. It's not one of the wars found in the Old Testament. This is a fight that involves Jesus. It's a supernatural slugfest, and it takes place in the desert after Jesus fasted for forty days, neither eating nor drinking during that time.[10]

His opponent is the ancient tempter commonly called the devil. He approaches the Son of God, ready for war, and his opening salvo is an invitation to turn stones into bread—a real enticement after more than a month with no food. Next, Satan seeks to lure Jesus into testing God, his Father, by jumping from the top of the temple and forcing the Father to save him by dispatching angels to catch him before he hits the ground. Then the devil launches his final attack. He promises Jesus all the splendor of the world's kingdoms—*if*. If Jesus will just bow down and worship him. It's a one-two-three punch, a barrage of temptation that comes pounding down while Jesus was weakened by hunger and thirst.

How Jesus responds is fascinating.

In each attack, he fights the temptation by speaking divine

truth, quoting from the book of Deuteronomy. (Deuteronomy is found in the Old Testament, the first part of the Bible.)

Each time, Jesus declared an unequivocal no!

No. I won't make bread in the desert to meet my own needs.

No. I won't force the Father to perform a circus act to prove his love.

No. I won't bow down to my enemy and take the easy path to power and authority.

No! No! No!

When Jesus was tempted, he quoted truth from the Bible. And if the devil tried to tempt Jesus (who was Immanuel, God in human flesh), you can be certain that you are not exempt from Satan's foul intentions.

Knowing we will face temptations, we would be wise to learn from Jesus' example and lock key Scripture verses into our heart.[11] When the enticement comes, we can respond with divine truth from the Bible.

Ask God for power to resist the temptations in your life and for help to overcome your negative patterns and habits. Enter this battle with words *and* actions as you learn to say no to temptation and yes to God and the life he wants for you.

In the coming chapters, you will find several examples of how to do this. One of the most effective ways you can say no is by memorizing powerful promises from the Bible that will enable you to respond at critical moments in your life.

49

NO NEGATIVITY

I grew up going to the movies. My mom loved the double features, and she would pack us into the car and bring us to the theater for special times together. When I think of my mom, I remember popcorn, Jujubes, soft drinks, and times spent together enjoying the latest movies on the silver screen.

For fifty years, I have followed the movie industry, observing their new offerings each year. One thing that has struck me over time, and has only accelerated over the past decade, is how increasingly difficult it is to find positive role models. Many of the heroes of today's cinema are not the kind of people you would want your children to model their lives after.

Many films today lack positive messages. Filmmakers enjoy portraying flaws, reveling in the depravity of our human condition. I make it a habit to visit *commonsensemedia.org* or other websites to check reviews before going to a movie. This site rates the things you would expect: violence, foul language, sex and nudity, drinking and drug use. And that's helpful.

But they also rate two other things: positive messages and positive role models. What is shocking is how low the scores are in these categories. More and more movies score a zero or one on a scale that goes to five.

Whereas I was raised going frequently to the movies, my wife grew up a world away. Her family never went to movies, and to this day she has little interest in them. When she evaluates something to watch, her first question is, "Is it edifying?" She wants to know, Is this good? Will it inspire? Are the characters noble? Will watching this make me a better person?

One of the ways marriage has changed me is by teaching me to make wiser decisions about what I set before my eyes. My wife has taught me to avoid the negative and to pursue the positive, both in life and in movies.

And as we have been discussing in this book, pursuing the positive means learning how to say no.

This lesson goes well beyond watching movies. Our conversations can become poisonous, gossipy, and critical. Say no to these. News coverage can quickly turn into propaganda, polarizing and hateful. Find something truly balanced or switch it off. Late-night talk shows can deteriorate into venomous diatribes. Say, "No more," and read a book instead. You get the idea.

Our world is filled with negativity and incivility, and these seem to be increasing exponentially. Here is my challenge. You can refuse the lure of pessimism, toxic attitudes, and never-ending negativism. Choose to fix your heart and mind on what is good, beautiful, positive, and edifying.

Don't just take my word for it. The Bible encourages us to pursue this attitude. Consider committing these words to memory:

Whatever is true, whatever is noble, whatever is right, whatever is pure, whatever is lovely, whatever is admirable—if anything is excellent or praiseworthy—think about such things.

—*Philippians 4:8*

50

NO BODY

Years ago, I had a profound realization.

If I could control everything that goes into my mouth, comes out of my mouth, and goes into my eyes, I would be a mature man!

I still believe this is true, and I am striving to achieve this goal.

I am not there yet.

In this chapter and the next two chapters, I want to look at each of these three areas in life. The first is learning how to control what goes into my mouth. This means watching what I eat and drink. It should be simple, right?

Just say no!

Do *not* make that stop at Taco Bell late at night. Do *not* open the freezer before bedtime to see if there is any ice cream. Do *not* venture down the snack aisle at the grocery store. Those bags of pretzels and tortilla chips always seem to jump right off the shelf and into the shopping cart.

The power of saying no is more than simply uttering the word. Along with the word must come consistent commitment and practices that affirm your declaration. Start by identifying the lies you tell yourself in these critical moments.

- "This will make me happy!"
- "It would be wrong to let it go to waste."
- "I deserve this."
- "I will start making better choices tomorrow."
- "I am starving!"
- "I need the energy."

The list is endless. We are amazingly creative in coming up with new excuses and justifying our behavior. In these moments, you must remind yourself that you have one body and it has to last your entire lifetime.

Care for it!

As you identify the lies and say no to body-damaging foods, you also need to make positive, healthy choices—over and over again. Say yes to good foods, modest portions, and boundaries. I confess this has been a lifelong battle for me. In my family as I was growing up, we ate when we were happy and celebrating, and we ate when we were down or discouraged. Every occasion was another good reason to consume more food.

I have learned that my body is a gift and I need to care for it. And I've had to say no hundreds, even thousands, of times. Slowly, healthy eating choices have become more natural for me.

Even now I must remain on guard.

Learn to care for your body. You will have to tell yourself no over and over, until making the right choices becomes natural for you. Once again, the Bible gives us help in saying no so that we can say yes to God's best for us. A powerful passage to fortify you in saying no to bad choices for your body is:

Do you not know that your bodies are temples of the Holy Spirit, who is in you, whom you have received from God? You are not your own; you were bought at a price. Therefore honor God with your bodies.

—1 Corinthians 6:19–20

51

NO WORDS

Words have power, more than most of us recognize. Some of our greatest moments of joy and meaning have come when someone spoke words of grace, love, and care.

- "I love you!"
- "Will you marry me?"
- "You are beautiful."
- "It's a girl!"
- "I forgive you."

Words can bring us to the heights of joy and make us feel glorious.

But they can also cut, wounding us deeply. You may have experienced your greatest heartache because of the words of another person. Often, those who are closest to us can pierce us with their words.

- "I hate you!"
- "I'm leaving you."

- "You are ugly."
- "I will never forgive you."
- "You are not welcome here."

Few things leave darker bruises on our heart and mind than harsh and mean-spirited words. In a collection of perhaps the best-known wise sayings ever recorded, we read these two proverbs:

- "The tongue has the power of life and death, and those who love it will eat its fruit" (Prov. 18:21).
- "The words of the reckless pierce like swords, but the tongue of the wise brings healing" (Prov. 12:18).

Few things in life are more destructive than unkind words. And if we are humble enough to admit it, our words have caused collateral damage in the hearts and lives of the people around us. This is why I encourage you to create a list of No Words.

What are No Words? These are predetermined statements, declarations, comments, threats, insults, or accusations that we know are toxic and dangerous. We decide—in advance of an emotionally charged moment—that we will never speak them.

I know married people who have made a commitment to never use the D word—divorce—when arguing with their spouse. They have banned that word because of its catastrophic ability to threaten the foundation of a marriage. I know a woman who has asked her husband to never use the word idiot while driving (especially when the kids are in the car). This was his go-to term for anyone who drove poorly (in his estimation). Some people have placed "I hate you" on their No Words list.

I would suggest putting the phrase "I could never forgive that" on every No Words list as well. I have chosen to put almost all profanity on my No Words list. I would rather stretch my mind and vocabulary to find more meaningful ways to express myself. Besides, I'm a pastor!

You can make your own list of words or sentences you never want to say. Write these down. Be specific! Reflect on the two proverbs I shared in this chapter, and commit to building a home, a workplace, a neighborhood, and friendships in which words no longer cut like sword thrusts and bring death. Bring healing and life through the things you say.

52

NO EYES

---✦---

A dear friend of mine served as a chaplain at two colleges for more than two decades. He had a unique, closeup view into the world of today's young adults. My friend would often say to me, "This might be the most unprotected generation in the history of the world."

Sadly, I have to agree.

Children and young people today are exposed to a wide and unfiltered array of ideas, attitudes, and images, most of which were formerly inaccessible or prohibited to younger minds. With the now-pervasive presence of the internet and with the proliferation of handheld devices, the world is at your fingertips.

When I was a child and into my teen years, I had to work very hard and be super-sneaky if I wanted to get my hands on even mildly inappropriate content. Today the worst of the worst is just one or two clicks away.

What was called pornography twenty years ago is now standard fare on cable networks, and college students watch and talk about these shows without blushing or any sense of impropriety. Hardcore porn is dangled before young people who spend a great deal of their time online. Few are able to escape these enticements.

What my chaplain friend said to describe college students a decade ago is true for all of us now. We live in an unprotected culture, one without boundaries, and it impacts each one of us. Every day, our eyes are exposed to unprecedented amounts of damaging material.

The problem is not going away, nor are things likely to improve anytime soon.

This is why you will need to learn how to say no to your eyes. We need to set boundaries for ourselves, because no one else will do it for us. This may sound countercultural, but wise people will make critical decisions about what they put in front of their eyes. What enters our eyes shapes our thoughts and forms our heart.

Some years ago, I attended a men's breakfast at which about one hundred men enjoyed great food and lively conversation. After breakfast, the speaker stood up and began his message. The topic was "Purity in an Impure World." His first question was both brilliant and piercing.

"If you have never struggled with pornography, will you raise your hand?"

How many hands do you think went up?

Not a single one.

No one in that group raised his hand to indicate that he had never struggled with pornography. In our world, both men and women must decide to say no to the tsunami of images and morally degrading content that is crashing over our culture.

This content dehumanizes women *and* men. It desensitizes the viewer to the real meaning and power of love and intimacy. We need to wake up and learn how to say no to our eyes, and we must teach the next generation how to have wisdom, boundaries, and discernment in this critical area.[12]

As a husband who loves his wife, a father who wants to be a good example for his sons, and a pastor who wants to live with integrity, I have developed my own ways of saying no to my eyes.

I've asked my cable company to remove some of the "free channels" that have movies and content I feel are inappropriate for me and my family. It wasn't easy! It took more than thirty minutes on the phone and an extra fee to have them take these channels off my package, but they were able to do it.

Whenever I travel for work and stay in a hotel room without my wife, I never turn on the TV. I know a leader who puts a towel over the TV and places a picture of his wife and family in front of it instead.

My computer belongs to the church I serve, and they have full access to all my search history and online activity. My wife and assistant know the passwords for my phone, tablet, and computer. I keep no secrets there. This accountability helps to keep me on the right path.

I try to stay away from places where my eyes will be exposed to things that I feel are unhealthy. Over the years, I have been invited to speak in the Netherlands on a number of occasions, and I've had friends say to me, "When you are in the Netherlands, you have to go to Amsterdam and see the red-light district." I've even had people offer to take me to this well-known neighborhood where selling people for sex is legal. Well-meaning people want me to see how bad it is.

I have said no on every occasion, not because I am trying to blind myself to the plight of those trapped in the sex trade. I say no to protect myself from seeing images I can never forget. I don't need to go on a voyeuristic field trip to see women and men for sale in shop windows to understand the brokenness of the human condition.

Saying no to my eyes is a conscious choice. Ultimately, the reason to say no is to free myself to say yes to the beauty and goodness in the world. I want my eyes locked on these things. Why waste your time filling your eyes, mind, and heart with damaging images that are difficult to erase? Err on the side of caution, and say no to your eyes when you are tempted to view anything inappropriate.

53

NO SEDUCTION

L ife is short. Have an affair."

This was the motto of the popular online dating service Ashley Madison, created for people who were married or in
an existing relationship. The model on the home page proudly
wore her wedding ring, even as she advertised herself available to
other men. This was a service designed to help people cheat—to
be unfaithful to those they claimed to love.

Sadly, sites like this one have only continued to grow in
popularity.

Ashley Madison hit the news several years ago when hackers
broke into the site and stole all of the customer data—names,
emails, financial information, and much more. Eventually,
much of this information was released to the public, and people
were shocked by the number of married men and women using
the site. Yet even after the public scandal, these kinds of sites
continue to draw people into unfaithful behavior.

Wise men and women learn to say no to the seductive enticements around them. Why compromise your marriage, family,

future, and integrity? If these things matter to you, set up clear boundaries that will protect your present and your future.

More than thirty years ago, I was studying for my master's degree. I was taking a psychology course and was assigned a project related to building healthy relationships. Since I was newly married, I chose to focus my study on the marriage relationship, and I wrote a paper about healthy boundaries that lead to lifelong faithfulness in marriage. In the paper, I listed my top ten personal rules, the nos I had established for myself in relating to women other than my wife. Here are a few of the guidelines I set up more than three decades ago and still follow today.

- Never go out for a meal one-on-one with a woman other than my wife or a family member.
- Never meet with a woman in my office with the door closed (unless there is a window in the door and people can see in).
- Never drive in the car alone with a woman besides my wife or a family member.

While my rules were all in reference to women, it is equally wise for women to set similar boundaries. These are all rules my wife follows regarding men.

After I presented my paper, a few of the students questioned me, offended and upset at the boundaries I had chosen to protect my marriage relationship. They accused me of being too severe.

"You're just afraid of your own sexuality!" one of them said to me.

To his surprise, I agreed with him. "You're right. I'm terrified of it! But in twenty years, I'll still be married and I'll still be a pastor. I'm not so sure about you!" Yes, I know that last comment was not necessary, but remember, I was still learning to say no to myself.

Let me be clear. I am not telling you to follow my rules. But I do encourage you to set boundaries that will protect your integrity, future, and family. I have seen so much pain and damage to men, women, and their children because of unfaithfulness. If you want to spare yourself and the people you love a world of pain and heartache, consider saying no to seduction. Start today by setting relational boundaries, and stick to them.[13]

54

NO TIME

While I was writing this book, I received a text from a leader I respect. He passed on a statistic about the video-streaming service Netflix: "Netflix Subscribers Streamed Record-Breaking 350 Million Hours of Video on Jan. 7, 2018."

He followed his text with this: "That's 39,954 years' worth of time."

I knew what he was saying. Earlier, we had been talking about how many people spend four, five, even six or more hours every day watching programs on demand on their televisions, computers, and handheld devices. There are seasons and seasons of streaming content. It's endless.

I often hear people say things like, "I have watched all seven seasons of [you name the series] three times!" They are excited, proud of their "accomplishment."

I find it sad.

Binge-watching is no longer seen as a waste of time; it's considered a normal part of life. I responded to my friend's text: "Wow . . . how sad! Wasted lives."

His reply was two words: "Pretty insane."

This is not a diatribe against watching TV programs or movies you might enjoy. My goal is to stir your thinking as you learn to set your priorities.

You and I have one life to live and a limited number of days on this planet. What I am suggesting is that we evaluate how we use our time. The problem is not just streaming movies and binge-watching television. There are many ways to entertain ourselves and distract ourselves with things that waste time and offer little in return.

Take a close look at your activities and habits. Your life may feel busy, but are you saying yes to time-wasters? Or are you saying yes to the things that matter most?

If you have no time, it may be time to say no to a habit or distraction that is whittling away your life.

NO CONCLUSION

NO REMINDERS

- Some nos are small and not all that significant, but others are massive and critical. You need to pay attention to the big nos.
- Our world might say there is no morality, but God disagrees! Saying no to things that hurt God and people leads to a moral and better life.
- Jesus said no to temptation. You can learn from his example.
- What goes into your mouth and what comes out of your mouth both really matter. Guard your mouth by saying no!
- Enticement and seduction will never go away. Identify where you need to say no to these. Then say no again and again.

NO EXERCISE

Do a study of your last month. Go back over your schedule and be brutally honest. How much time did you spend watching TV or other media? What else did you spend a lot of time doing that might not have been the wisest use of your hours and days? Figure out how much time you can get back if you say no to some of these activities. (This does not mean you never do them, but trim out some of the hours if they are excessive.) Then allocate this time to doing some of the important things you want to say yes to.

PART

6

NO

RESULTS

Saying no is hard, but it's worth the pain. The benefits will soon begin to surface as you learn to live in the world of no. Don't get weary. Hang in there!

While training for a big hike, a marathon, or a triathlon, you may need to say no a hundred times to avoid distractions and temptations. But when you get to the pinnacle or cross the finish line, there is nothing like it.

If you want to be a great parent, you will have to say no countless times to your children. Friends and coworkers will invite you to join them for fun experiences, but sometimes you will turn them down because you have commitments with your kids. You will feel pulled to work extra hours, but the needs of your family will come first. There will be enticements for all sorts of "me time," but love for your children will help you say no to me and yes to them.

Saying no to these and other distractions will be worth it someday when your kids are older and declare that they love and respect you. They will remember how you were present and engaged in their lives. They will recognize and appreciate the sacrifices you made. Then you will be profoundly thankful that you said all those nos. But you might have to wait for your kids to get past adolescence!

A lifetime of nos leads to life filled with yes.

55

NO UNDERSTANDING

I have practiced saying no for about three decades, and over the years I've watched how people respond when they are told no.

Even when I've said no in a thoughtful and clear manner, using the correct no from my menu of options, about 10 percent of the people have not liked it! They push back, express dissatisfaction with me, and try to get me to become a compliant person who always does what they want.

Don't let the frustration or anger of the 10 percent control your life. Hold your ground.

Here is what I have discovered. As I've embraced a life of healthy boundaries, prioritizing what matters most, about 80 percent of the people get it. When I say no with clarity and kindness, the vast majority of people respect my decision and don't push back at all. These folks don't say much but simply embrace my new boundary. Most people won't mind when you say no. Some will hardly notice!

Here is what I've enjoyed the most. About one out of every ten people who receive a no from me will ask honest questions and want to learn more. They aren't used to someone saying no with confidence and clarity in a polite and respectful way. There are people who will appreciate your conviction and may even want to be more like you. With people like this, you have an opportunity! Teach them what you have learned about the beauty of no.

No matter how others respond, choose to stay the course. Your future and your life depend on it!

56

NO NOS

---✵---

As you learn to say no confidently and regularly, you will discover that there are times when you don't have to say no at all. You'll identify situations in which you can say a positive yes or a series of yeses. Because you understand the wisdom and power of a well-spoken no, you are aware that there are times when you do not need to say this beautiful word.

I call this a No Nos moment.

Some years ago, I had the privilege of playing one of the most famous golf courses in the world, the Old Course at St. Andrews, Scotland. It happened to be a cold day, in the low forties. The wind was blowing a sustained twenty miles an hour and gusting up to thirty miles an hour. Because of the severe conditions, one of the golfers in our group decided not to play. He had hired a top-level professional caddie named Stewart and had already paid the caddie fee and a good tip.

My friend told me and one of our buddies that we could each use this amazing caddie for nine holes. We later learned that Stewart worked for an Irish professional golfer most of the year and caddied at St. Andrews in his off-season.

We met Stewart on the first tee, and I knew right away he was an absolute pro. He did something I had never experienced before. He walked over to my golf bag, took out my driver, looked me straight in the eye, and asked (with a very cool Irish accent), "What can you do with your driver?"

I told him how far I could hit it and the various shots I could make. He went on, pulling out every club in my bag and asking me questions about how I hit each one of them. Then he handed me my putter and said, "We tee off in about ten minutes; go over there and practice putting for five minutes."

I was a little shocked at his directness, but I did what I was told. He was the pro!

When I came back to the first tee, my caddie handed me my five-wood and said, "Hit the ball as hard as you like toward the Swilcan Bridge. You will think you are too far left, but the angle is perfect."

He pointed at the bridge that was actually on the eighteenth hole. I did what he said, and he was spot on. When we got to my ball, he handed me a pitching wedge and told me to hit it on the very front of the green.

"It will bounce all the way back to the flag," he said. And he was right again!

I could tell this was a perfect No Nos moment. I looked at this man and realized he knew the golf course far better than I did. The conditions were vicious, but he understood the nuances of playing in the strong Scottish costal wind in a way I never would. I decided that for the first nine holes, while he was my caddie, I would do exactly what he told me to do. I would not disagree, push back, or say no to any of his suggestions. At that point, I trusted him more than I trusted myself.

That day, my friends struggled in the cold and the wind. One of them is a great golfer, and in normal conditions he would have been three or four strokes over par. That day, he was almost twenty strokes over par when we finished the front nine.

I played the best nine holes of my life. The conditions were challenging, but I said yes to every instruction my caddie gave me. When we made the turn, I was disappointed that Stewart was leaving me to carry my friend's clubs for the back nine.

As we walked to the tenth tee, my friend did something amazingly kind. He came over and said, "You're shooting a great round, aren't you?"

"I'm only two over par," I replied. "This isn't the lowest score I've ever shot for nine holes, but it's the best golf I've ever played!"

He looked at me and said, "You keep the caddie. I suck!"

I asked him if he was sure. He held up his scorecard, pointed at his abysmal score, and told me to finish the round with Stewart.

On the back nine, I continued my No Nos philosophy, saying yes to every suggestion Stewart made. He handed me the clubs and told me what shots to make. I never picked a club and never told him no. Even in terrible conditions, it was my finest round of golf ever.

As you get better at knowing when and how to say no, there will come those rare times when you do not need to say it at all. In those times, as you place your trust in another and open yourself to fully embrace the moment, continue saying yes.

57

NO FUN

━━━◦━━━

When you learn to say no, one of the wonderful results is that life becomes more fun. You spend a whole lot less time doing things because of guilt or pressure. You make space for what matters most.

For twenty years, my wife and I went on annual family vacations with our three boys. These experiences were incredibly fun, almost beyond description. We laughed, played, shared meals, took hikes, skied, went places with friends, boated, sat by roaring fires, played tennis, lounged around, swam, and laughed some more. I would not trade these memories for anything!

But here is the reality. We *never* left for vacation with everything done. There were still chores on our checklist. Life was never in perfect order. It would have been easy to postpone things until we could get everything done. Instead we had to say no to the never-ending tasks and obligations so we could say yes to family time and memories that will last a lifetime.

Almost every evening for the past ten years, my wife and I have played at least one game of backgammon or cribbage. We both work hard, and we have offices in our home. There are always demands, things crying out for our time and attention. It would be easy to cycle from work to sleep and back to work, never taking time to slow down or play.

But what kind of life would that be?

We make sure that at least once, most evenings, we push aside the demands of life and the expectations others have of us and just have a little fun. We chat, we laugh, and we play games.

And I get beat a lot.

Every two weeks, the people on the staff I lead have lunch together. We consider this part of our workweek, so our hourly people are paid for this time. As we sit at the tables, sharing a meal, there is conversation, laughter, and engagement in one another's lives. A passerby might wonder if this is a good use of our time.

I would say absolutely.

It is healthy and even necessary to have fun. Having fun builds community and creates cohesion in a group. Every person on our staff has work they could be doing, but for a time we all say no to the daily responsibilities in order to spend forty-five minutes of fun time together.

Learning to say no means making space for fun, for human connection, and for time to play and enjoy being with others.

58

NO REST

G od created us. He knows best how we operate.

In his divine wisdom, God has hardwired us for work *and* for rest. There is a rhythm to the universe and to our bodies, and it was placed there by the One who designed us.

It's not complicated. Work six days, rest one day. The following week, work six, rest one. The next week . . .

You get the picture.

The day of rest is called the Sabbath. It is an ancient practice modeled by God and rooted in the natural, created order. It was reiterated to the world in the Ten Commandments, and it leads to health, life, and productivity.

Stop and think for a moment. The Creator of the universe made you and me, and he tells us to take a day off every week, a day away from our normal pattern of work and striving. In the ancient world, the economy was based on agricultural productivity, and taking a day away from labor was unheard of for most people, in particular the poor. Even today, there are those who must work two or three jobs just to make ends meet. Many of them work seven days a week without rest.

The Sabbath day is a gift for us. Our Creator knows we will be more productive working six days and resting one. You will never get more accomplished by working seven days a week. The gift of the Sabbath increases our joy, our rest, and our productivity.

Some years ago, I accepted a challenge to compete in a triathlon. A buddy of mine gave me a book written by a successful triathlete, and in a chapter discussing his training, the author wrote about a strange phenomenon he had observed. He explained that many people, as they train consistently, get addicted to the rhythm of swimming, cycling, and running. They find they want to get out and train every day. He suggested that it is better for triathletes to train six days and take a full day off each week.

Over the years, he had noticed that the race times of athletes were worse if they trained every day with no rest. If they rested just one day a week, their race times improved, and they were able to perform at a higher level.

I'll never forget his conclusion at the end of the chapter. He was baffled. It made no sense to him at all, even though he knew it was true.

But this makes perfect sense if we listen to the One who created us! Of course triathletes perform better with one day off a week; that's how our bodies were designed. God has made us for hard work *and* deep rest. We need both.

If you want to live your life at the next level, decide to embrace God's rhythm of life and make regular rest a priority by saying no to your labor one day every week.

Dare to try this. For the next four weeks, do your best to take a full day off every seven days. Even turn your phone off or block all calls from the office. Don't check your work email on that day. It might be painful at first. At the end of four weeks, evaluate how you feel and your productivity level. I predict that you will be pleasantly surprised.

59

NO ENERGY

Saying yes to every opportunity, invitation, and demand on your life is flat-out exhausting! If you are a Yes Machine, you know exactly what I mean.

It leads to energy depletion on a physical, emotional, and relational level. You feel you just can't keep pushing forward at this pace. You might even dream about cutting back, slowing down, or giving up.

One of the greatest results of learning to say thoughtful nos on a consistent basis is that your energy comes back. You wake up more refreshed. You go through your day feeling motivated rather than just surviving another twenty-four hours. You start to dream fresh new dreams for your life because you have energy to imagine new things.

Saying no may feel difficult and exhausting at first. But over time, your batteries will be recharged. You will replenish your energy reserves.

60

NO THINKING

I met Jack almost three decades ago. He worked as an editor at a publishing company, and he hired me for my first writing project. We immediately became far more than colleagues. We became friends.

When I learned that he loved to golf, I invited him out for a round at a local course. There are few things I find more enjoyable than getting outdoors for a couple hours, walking a golf course, and having a great conversation with an interesting person.

On the first tee, I saw something I had never seen before. I watched this brilliant man stand over his golf ball and go through a series of physical contortions as he practiced swinging, preparing to hit the ball. It looked like he had a dozen different thoughts going through his mind, like he was trying to wrestle his body into a routine of movement that was utterly foreign to him.

I did something that might have seemed a bit rude. I interrupted him.

"Jack, before you hit your ball, can I ask you something?"

Instead of being annoyed, he seemed relieved as he stepped away from his ball. I asked him a simple question.

"What are you thinking as you stand over the ball and get ready to hit?"

He began talking about a video he had watched to learn to turn away from the ball just right. Then he mentioned an article he had read about some type of body rotation he was trying to replicate. Next, he shared details about a book he was reading by a golf pro, who offered a great tip that would add ten yards to his tee shot.

After he explained four or five ideas he was trying to incorporate into his swing, I asked him, "How many things are you thinking about as you get ready to hit the ball?"

He said, "Nine."

I was feeling wound up myself!

He asked me, "Do you have some swing thoughts you use as you hit the ball?"

I feared he was looking to add a tenth idea to his complex process. But I decided to share with him what goes through my mind just before I make a golf swing.

I said three words. "Do that again!"

He stared at me with a blank look. "What are you talking about?"

I paused. "Jack, I have only one thought as I hit a golf ball. It is very simple. I think, *Do that again*. Sometimes I even say it out loud before I swing. That's it!"

Jack looked confused.

I explained that I try to relax while making a golf swing. I stand near my ball and make a few easy practice swings. When the swing feels really comfortable, I step up to my ball, make sure I'm pointing in the right direction, and think, *Do that again*.

It's nothing fancy. Just basic muscle memory. I take a simple thought and try to repeat that smooth practice swing. Thankfully, most of the time it works fairly well. I'm just duplicating a practice swing that felt good and natural.

I'm not trying to give you a golf lesson.

My point is that there are times, just like that moment before my golf swing, when I must say no to a thousand other thoughts. I must simplify, so I isolate one idea and go with it. When I say no to all the other thoughts, I can say yes to the one that needs to rule my mind at that moment.

The practice of saying no to extra thoughts is what I mean by No Thinking. You aren't clearing your mind of all thought. You are clearing it of all but one idea. This way you can say yes to what matters most in that moment, the thing you want to focus on.

When I am at work, I say no to thinking about the rest of my life. Thoughts that could divide my focus are pushed away for that time. I don't think about what I will do later. I don't think about spending time with my wife and kids or hanging out with my friends. I say no to all of those thoughts. This may sound heartless and unkind, but it is not, I assure you.

It leads to amazing productivity! .

If an emergency comes up, I can shift gears quickly to focus on family, friends, or whatever hits my radar.

It makes sense to stop thinking about the rest of my world while I'm at work. This discipline frees me to focus exclusively on my family when I am with them. When I am having social time and fun with friends, I seek to be fully present there. I am committed to focus on who I'm with and what I'm doing at that moment.

Some people call this being present or mindful or focused. I call it No Thinking. If you work at it, it's not that hard to learn and even master. Practice being present. Let your mind stay focused on one thing, one person, or one swing thought.

In our wired and distracted world, this discipline may require you to turn off your phone or anything that buzzes, beeps, or otherwise clamors for your attention. These devices will keep your mind fragmented and distracted.[14]

In case you are wondering, my buddy Jack decided to forget his other swing thoughts that day. For nine holes, he focused on one phrase: "Do that again."

He shot one of the best nine holes of his life.

61

NO CLUTTER

———✳———

Cornell University did a study on the impact of clutter on an individual's psychological well-being. In particular, researchers looked at how kitchen clutter impacted snacking.

Yes, people actually study these things.[15]

Here is what they did. The researchers had some subjects cook in a kitchen that was clean and tidy. Another group of subjects cooked in the same kitchen, but it was strewn with mail, papers, and other objects. In both cases, the same snacks were made available to the cooks.

What did the researchers learn?

The cooks in the cluttered kitchen ate 44 percent more snacks than did the cooks in the tidy kitchen. Dr. Wansink concluded, "If your environment is out of control, you may feel that you don't need to be in control of your eating either."

One benefit of growing in your ability to say no is that you can live a less cluttered life. Why? Because when you master the discipline of saying no in one area, it will increase your discipline in other areas. You can learn to say no to yourself. You can stop buying things you don't need and have nowhere to put.

You can say no to keeping objects that clutter your home, office, garage, and car.

You can look at all your stuff and say, "If I don't have room for you, out you go!"

My oldest son, Zach, and his wife, Christine, were preparing to move. They knew they didn't want to pack and transport things they didn't need, so they used this time of transition to rigorously examine all they owned.

They asked, "Do we really need this?"

They embraced simplicity, striving for a more spartan approach to living. They set a goal of giving away stuff every day for thirty days. On day one, they gave away one thing. On day two, they had to find two things to donate to a good cause. Every day for thirty days, they kept giving away more things. On the final day, they gave away thirty items![16]

Zach and Christine had been married only a few years. They live far more simply than most couples I know. Yet at the end of this month-long journey, they had given away well over four hundred things! When it was over, they both said, "This was fun and freeing. And it wasn't that hard!"

They said no to more stuff, and they decluttered their home and life.

If the folks at Cornell are right, they probably snacked a lot less too!

62

NO PRIORITIES

People who can't seem to say no have a hard time keeping their priorities in order. The reason is obvious. When we say yes to everything, our priorities get buried under a fresh pile of new responsibilities. All of these new obligations—especially the ones that scream, "Urgent!"—end up taking precedence over the commitments we have already made. The urgent will always win over the mundane, unless we set clear priorities.

As we learn to say no to the things that are not critical, we have time for what matters most. We can establish routines and keep our priorities front and center. Make a list of those simple but essential priorities in your life. Here are some suggestions from the lives of people close to me.

- Make a to-do list every morning and use it.
- Make my bed each morning.
- Read the Bible and talk with God a bit (pray).
- Exercise at least five days a week.
- Have a conversation with each of my kids on a daily basis.

- Straighten my office before I go home for the day.
- Floss every night before bed.
- Have a date with my spouse every week or two.
- Pay my bills and review my finances at the end of each month.
- Wash my car and check the fluid levels and tire pressure at least once a month.
- Call my parents at least once a week to see how they are doing.

None of these are earth-shattering. Most are quite commonplace. But as we follow through on the simple priorities of life, we establish patterns of daily, weekly, and monthly consistency that make us who we are. If we refuse to say no to the urgent and often unnecessary things that are always trying to muscle into our schedule, they will take over and push out our routines and priorities.

When this happens, our whole life can get thrown out of whack.

Learn to say no in order to focus on your daily priorities, those habits and rhythms that keep life on pace and make you the person you want to become.

63

NO WAY

Throughout history, people have established guidelines and rules to create a way of life for themselves and their communities. In the sixth century, Benedict of Nursia established a standard for those who wanted to live as monks in the Benedictine order. It included commitments to live a life of chastity, poverty, fidelity, obedience.

Pretty serious stuff!

All of this was written down, and the rules guided every person who chose to belong to this order.

That was fifteen hundred years ago.

More recently, pastor and evangelist Billy Graham wrote more than thirty books and, over seven decades of ministry, called people to a certain way of life. He invited them to follow Christ, which involved things like reading the Bible, praying, attending church, sharing the story of Jesus, obeying God's commands, and living wholesomely.

With both Benedict and Billy, we can identify a personal way of life—patterns they established that were essential for health and vitality. Walking in this way of life and earnestly pursuing the markers of maturity became a daily passion and pursuit for these men and for those who modeled their lives after them.

I find there is wisdom in establishing a way of life that embraces the beauty of no. As we close this section, I want to challenge you to come up with three to five clear indications of what it will mean for you to live in the No Way.

Here are some ideas to get the wheels turning.

No Way of Life

- I will seek to recognize that every time I say yes to one thing, I am almost always saying no to something else.
- I will seek to develop a wide menu of nos and will practice saying them until I can do so with ease and kindness.
- I will say no even when it is scary, hard, or dangerous.
- I will always use the gentlest no possible to accomplish the task, and I will try to do it with a smile and a kind heart.
- I will pay attention to the many benefits of saying no and learn to recognize the high cost of saying yes when I should have said no.
- I will use the word no to help me resist temptation, grow in morality, and build a healthy and whole life.
- I will say no as often as I need to so I can say yes to the things that matter most in life.
- I will grow in my awareness that no is a beautiful word.

NO CONCLUSION

NO REMINDERS

- Saying no is hard, but it is even harder to live with the results of saying yes when you should have said no!
- When you begin saying no, some people will push back, but most people will respect your decision to set healthy boundaries.
- When you become skilled at saying no, you will recognize that there are many situations in which you do not need to say it.
- When you get into the rhythm of saying no with grace and wisdom, life will be more fun, and you will find yourself more rested and living with greater energy reserves.
- Saying no can help you unclutter your mind, your home, and your life.
- Learning to say no will free you to pursue the priorities that make life worth living.

NO EXERCISE

Write three to five simple statements that will become the beginning of your No Way of life. Share these with someone you trust and love.

PART

7

THE
FREEDOM OF
YES

The title of this book captures the idea I want you to believe and embrace. No is a beautiful word. It has beauty because if you say it consistently and wisely, it frees you to say an even more beautiful word.

Yes!

As you establish a meaningful No Way of life, you will begin to experience this freedom. You'll find lots of room for those yeses.

You are now free to say yes to the things that matter most.

Yes to the people you love.

Yes to the things you enjoy.

Yes to the doors God opens.

Yes to generosity with your time and resources.

Yes to spontaneously serving others.

Yes to an occasional nap.

Yes to being positive and encouraging.

Yes to faithfulness in your relationships.

Yes to priorities that lead to a rich life.

Yes to the life you have always dreamed of.

64

THOUGHTFUL YES

As your life begins to shift into new and healthy patterns, be sure you are thoughtful about your yeses. As I warned earlier, don't make the mistake of becoming a Yes Machine. If you do, your life will shift right back to the overextended, insanely busy, out-of-control prison you just escaped.

Learn to utter a thoughtful yes.

Here are four questions you should ask as you consider saying yes to new opportunities.

"What will this yes cost?" Every yes has a price tag. Even the best yes costs something. Be honest, think it through, name it. There can be a cost of time (and we almost always underestimate this). There is emotional cost. Think about financial implications. A thoughtful yes involves acknowledging the costs and then committing to make the investment. If you can't count the cost, don't say the yes!

"What will I have to set aside to follow through on this yes?" Most of the best and rewarding yeses in life involve setting something else aside or cutting back on other things. A yes to marriage will change your relational life a bit! Yes to starting a

family has massive impact, and some things will get pushed to the back burner, potentially for years. Taking a new job, starting a degree program, even taking up a new hobby will all demand a lifestyle adjustment.

To be crystal clear, these big yeses are worth the sacrifice. But we should not say the yes without being aware that our lives will change. There will be sacrifice. And it will be glorious!

"Can I take baby steps into this yes?" There are many yeses that can be entered into with little steps. You do not have to jump in with both feet and overwhelm yourself. Suppose you have a daughter and someone asks if you can coach her soccer team. Why not say, "I've never done that. Can I be a helper for a year, learn more about the sport, and see if this fits me?" Take a step into that world without taking full responsibility for the team from the first day.

"Will this yes lead to a good, healthy, and meaningful life?" You can predict the future with a fair level of accuracy if you thoughtfully ponder the implications of the yes you are about to make. Before you say yes, stop and reflect on what this will mean for your life in a day, week, month, or even a year.

Is there a good chance this yes will just waste your time and spin you in needless directions? Then don't say yes! Are you fairly sure this yes will lead to a better life, better health for you and others, and deeper meaning? If so, you can be much more confident when you say yes!

65

STRATEGIC YES

How do you say a strategic yes? It begins with knowing your priorities. When you are clear about what matters most, you can easily determine each yes and no. If you aren't confident about your priorities, it will be almost impossible to make a decision.

"What are my relational priorities?" "What do I value most financially?" "Do I have clear and defined spiritual priorities?" "How do I want to use my free time?" "What are my goals for my education and vocation?" These and similar questions will help you determine what is worth a yes and what is a waste of time and energy.

I can't tell you what your priorities should be. That is for you to determine. I would suggest that the best and most important step in clarifying your life mission is to talk with the God who made you.

Spend time talking with those closest to you as well, asking them what they see in you. Are there any gifts or talents that are uniquely yours? Ask them, "When do you see me come alive?" It will help you identify your passions. Find someone who can help you dream. Think about the kind of person you want to be. What changes do you need to make to be that person?

Your priorities will shape your yeses and your nos.

If your aspiration is to make as much money as you can, no matter what you have to do or who you have to use, and then to spend all of your money on self-pleasure and indulgence, your yeses will be determined by this set of priorities. On the other hand, if your goal is to earn a living doing something you love, in partnership with people you enjoy, and to pay your bills, save enough to help others, and have a reasonable retirement, your yeses will look quite different.

If your highest priority is to watch every season of every show that is available on demand, you will say some very specific yeses. On the other hand, if your priority is to use your extra time to enjoy friendships and serve the under-resourced in your community, I am pretty sure you will say yes to a dramatically different list of things.

Think through what you value most. Then establish priorities that will help you put first things first. Once you have done this, make sure you say yes in a strategic manner. Every yes should help you move closer to what matters most in your life.

CHAPTER

66

REFLEXIVE YES

———✳———

One of the best ways to save time and propel yourself forward in saying yes to the right things is to determine specific moments when you will say a reflexive yes. This is a yes that you determine to use before you encounter the situation.

This is not to say you would not stop to think, ponder, or pray. What it means is that there are times when you set your default on yes (unless there is a good reason not to).

When I see a person in genuine need and I am able to help, I will say yes.

When someone asks me a direct question, I will say yes to speaking the truth.

When one of my kids reaches out to me, I will say yes to making time to connect with them.

When someone asks me to give a small amount to a charity, I will say an excited yes.

A few years ago, at Christmastime, I got irritated at all of the people asking for a few dollars for their particular charity. I would be in a restaurant paying the bill, and the server would say, "Would you like to donate a dollar to cancer research?"

As I paid for groceries, the cashier would say, "May we round your bill up to the nearest dollar to help orphans have a better Christmas?" I noticed every Salvation Army bell ringer standing near the entrance at the mall. It bugged me that everywhere I went, people were asking for more.

I am embarrassed to say it, but I was constantly irritated.

Then I had a change of heart. Instead of focusing on the annoyance of constant requests, I decided, I would say yes every time someone made a modest appeal. Why not embrace it and joyfully and enthusiastically say yes to these opportunities to be generous?

From that point on, when someone asked me, "Would you like to give a little toward—" I would cut them off before they finished the sentence. "I would love to!" It became a game. I think people have grown so used to hearing cynical nos that I startled them with my enthusiasm. I began to hear expressions of gratitude.

"Thanks! You're the first person today!"

"Wow, that is really nice!"

I made my giving in these small amounts a reflexive and automatic yes. And once I did this, a number of things changed for me. First, my attitude took a 180-degree turn. Instead of being a grumpy Scrooge, I radiated joy. My attitude became contagious and uplifting. It inspired the people who were asking for donations. I realized that many of them had a difficult job, and this was an opportunity to bless them in their thankless work. Every cause I encountered received a small donation. At the end of the season, I realized that I had given about thirty-nine dollars over a six-week period. It was one of the best investments of money I've ever made, and I've continued making this a reflexive yes every Christmas since then.

I look forward to it.

67

LET YOUR YES BE YES

More than two thousand years ago, the wisest teacher who ever walked on this planet gave the most famous speech in history. He was talking to a large group of people on a mountainside. There were academics and elites. And the poor and outcast of the day were gathered as well. In his Sermon on the Mount, Jesus addressed many topics. One of them was the importance of saying what we mean and making sure we mean what we say. He said it this way: "Make sure your yes is a yes and your no is a no" (Matt. 5:33–37, my paraphrase; the key verse is 37).

In other words, when you say yes, mean it.

And if you have to say no, say it with conviction, and follow through.

People should know you are as good as your word.

68

GOD YES

I grew up in a loving and healthy home, but we had no religious traditions or practices to guide our family life. I didn't realize Christmas and Easter were religious holidays. Santa Claus, the Easter Bunny, family, and food were the beginning and end of these celebrations. I had no religious or faith framework.

I did not know whether God existed.

I didn't really care.

Then I had a series of encounters with people who had a genuine relationship with God through faith in Jesus Christ. Their lives had a profound effect on me. They had meaning and joy in ways I had not experienced or even contemplated. They had a clear purpose for living. They said no to certain things so they could say yes to God. This radical mindset was not just the result of some mystical conversion experience in their past. It guided every choice they made in their present.

I was intrigued. I began to wonder if maybe there was something to the Christian faith.

What if it was true that God existed and loved us?

What if human beings were separated from God, not because of his distance but because of our own rebellion?

What if Jesus really did enter human history to build a bridge back to the heart of his Father?

What if a whole new life could begin because of a decision to confess personal wrongs and embrace the love and grace of Jesus? What if it was possible to take the hand of God, follow him, and lead an amazing new kind of life?

Could this be true?

Could a yes to God make all the difference in my life and throughout eternity?

After years of saying no to God through apathy and rebellion, I finally said, "God, yes!" I confessed my wrongs to God and accepted the amazing grace Jesus offered me through his sacrifice on the cross.

That one yes has made all the difference in the world. It has changed the trajectory of my life and my future, forever.

My first "God, yes" has led to countless other identical declarations that have propelled me to a life I never would have imagined possible.

If you have never said yes to God, I encourage you to prayerfully consider doing so. There is no greater yes you can make.

He loves you.

He knows you.

He left heaven and died on a cross to show you his love and to make a way for you to come home to him. He rose from the dead and is alive today! He has a plan for the rest of your life. His arms are open, and he is waiting.

If you have already said, "Yes, God," and embraced the love and grace of Jesus, keep saying, "Yes, God"! Let your daily reflexive yes be, "Your will be done."

Whatever God calls you to do and however he calls you to live, say yes.

FEASTING ON THE YES

We began our journey sixty-eight chapters ago in the book introduction. (I hope you read it.) We started at a buffet with a plate so jammed full of food that there was no room for anything else. This is a picture of a life so overloaded that things are falling off the plate.

The philosopher Forrest Gump once famously said, "Life is like a box of chocolates; you never know what you're gonna get."

I have my own twist on that. Life is like a buffet, and there is always more than you can fit on your plate. If you never say no, your plate will be overloaded. Your life will feel frenzied, your schedule will be out of control, your body will be exhausted, and your spirit will be numb.

This is not a good way to live.

The single most important lesson of this book is to understand that as you learn to walk down the buffet of life and confidently say no to many of the options, you will begin to make room on your plate. You will be free to say yes to the best options.

Your priorities will snap back into focus. Your margin will return. You will begin to play again, laugh again, and experience peace again. Your relationships will blossom and flourish.

This is the kind of life we all long for, and it is the kind of life God wants you to experience.

As you walk down the buffet of life, I hope you will learn that no is a beautiful word. Say it often. Speak it well. And mean it when you say it. But never forget that as beautiful as it is to say no, there is an even greater beauty in the freedom to say yes. May your life be a feast of saying yes to all that God has planned for you.

Bon appetit!

NOTES

1. The Billy Graham Center for Evangelism was using my books *Organic Outreach for Ordinary People* and *Organic Outreach for Churches*. For more information, see *Organicoutreach.org*.
2. This book is published by Zondervan and is an easy read.
3. *https://worldmission.cc*.
4. For more information on Organic Outreach International, see *https://organicoutreach.org*.
5. You can find this article at *www.kevingharney.com* under resources and articles.
6. Dr. James Dobson has written about this topic, but there is also a helpful video that gets to the heart of the idea: *www.lightsource.com/ministry/family-talk-videos/saying-no-to-our-children-483068-full.html*.
7. It is called the *Seniors' Devotional Bible* and was published by Zondervan.
8. Check out this study, especially the section on how smiling affects those around you: *www.psychologytoday.com/us/blog/cutting-edge-leadership/201206/there-s-magic-in-your-smile*.
9. Malcolm Gladwell, *Blink: The Power of Thinking without Thinking*.
10. To dig into this topic, take time to read Matthew 4:1–11 and Luke 4:1–13.
11. Jesus quoted from the Old Testament book of Deuteronomy each time he battled the tempter in

Matthew 4 and Luke 4. You can find great passages in the Old and New Testaments on almost any topic. Just do a quick search on the internet for "What the Bible says about . . ." and fill in the blank.

12. You might want to look at the book *Every Man's Battle* by Stephen Arterburn and Fred Stoeker.

13. You might want to read and reflect on Proverbs 5–7.

14. You might want to read *Deep Work: Rules for Focused Success in a Distracted World* by Cal Newport.

15. Learn more about the Cornell study at *https://foodpsychology.cornell.edu/discoveries/clean-kitchens-cut-calories.*

16. You might want to read Jeff Manion's book *Satisfied: Discovering Contentment in a World of Consumption.*

Organic Outreach
BOOKS

Kevin Harney offers the tools needed to reach out with God's love in organic ways. In these resources, you will discover that sharing the good news of Jesus can be as natural as talking about your favorite sports team or telling a friend about a wonderful new restaurant. On the golf course, over coffee, while taking a walk—anywhere and everywhere—become a bearer of grace. Share the amazing love of God. Tell the life-changing story of Jesus. Discover ordinary ways to communicate God's love and the message of salvation naturally.

9780310566106: Organic Outreach for Ordinary People
9780310566076: Organic Outreach for Churches
9780310273974: Organic Outreach for Families

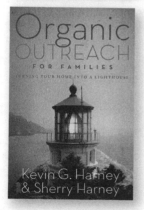

Organic Outreach
DVDs

In these practical video studies, Kevin Harney offers the tools needed to reach out with God's love in organic ways. You will also learn how to multiply the outreach and impact of your church by weaving evangelism into the fabric of your church.

9780310537694: Organic Outreach for Churches DVD
9780310531197: Organic Outreach DVD

OrganicOutreach

INTERNATIONAL

Through training, coaching, and provision of resources, Organic Outreach International is committed to helping denominations, national groups, regional movements, parachurch organizations, and local churches around the world infuse the DNA of their ministries and congregations with a passion for natural evangelism. We offer online and onsite training sessions ranging from half-day introductory seminars to two-day Intensive Trainings. For churches and movements that are directly engaging in organic outreach, we provide a collaborative coaching experience for small groups (cohorts) of pastors and Outreach Influence Team Leaders through a combination of online work and monthly video-conferencing.

For churches and organizations engaging in organic outreach, we provide free resources on our website. As you browse through this library, you will find a full three years of Outreach Influence Team meeting agendas, samples of Level 3 to Level 4 Influence plans, an Outreach Influence Team Leader ministry description, training and informational videos, and more. We are constantly updating and adding to these tools, so check back often.

You can contact the OOI team through the website (www .OrganicOutreach.org) or by email (info@OrganicOutreach.org).

Organic Outreach International is a ministry of Shoreline Community Church in Monterey, California.